Moira Watson was born i  when she was nine. Here governesses for school a degree that was interrup four years in the Navy's ____ ___ ____ ____, included being the first publicity officer for the Melbourne Zoo; she has written poems and stories all her life. She is married and has two daughters and a son, and still lives in Melbourne. *Razzle Dazzle* is her first set of memoirs; *The Keeper of the Nest*, coming out in September, is her first novel.

MW00912739

IMPRINT

RAZZLE DAZZLE

MOIRA WATSON

ANGUS
& ROBERTSON

AN ANGUS & ROBERTSON BOOK

First published in Australia in 1990 by
Collins/Angus & Robertson Publishers Australia

Collins/Angus & Robertson Publishers Australia
Unit 4, Eden Park, 31 Waterloo Road, North Ryde,
NSW 2113, Australia

Collins/Angus & Robertson Publishers New Zealand
31 View Road, Glenfield, Auckland 10, New Zealand

Angus & Robertson (UK)
16 Golden Square, London WIR 4BN, United Kingdom

Copyright © Moira Watson 1990

This book is copyright.
Apart from any fair dealing for the purposes of
private study, research, criticism or review, as
permitted under the Copyright Act, no part may be
reproduced by any process without written permission.
Inquiries should be addressed to the publishers.

National Library of Australia
Cataloguing-in-Publication data

Watson, Moira, 1922–
Razzle dazzle.

ISBN 0 207 16678 1.

1. Watson, Moira, 1922–   – Childhood and youth. 2.
Hobart (Tas.) – Social life and customs – 1922–1945. 3.
Melbourne (Vic.) – Social life and customs – 1922–1939.
I. Title.

920.72

Typeset in Sydney by Deblaere Typesetting Pty Ltd
Printed in Australia by Globe Press

Cover photograph: Razzle Dazzle 1908, by Harold Cazneaux
gelatin silver photograph
22.4 x 28.4cm
Gift of the Cazneaux family
Art Gallery of New South Wales

Angus & Robertson's creative writing programme is assisted by the Australia Council, the
Australian governments arts advisory and support organisation.

5   4   3   2   1
95 94 93 92 91 90

For Peter
Jane, Amanda and Peter Jonathon,
and for 'Bubba', my sister Lesley
who shares many of these memories.

My thanks to Carmel Bird
who started me on this voyage of discovery
into the past.

Ever drifting down the stream
Lingering in the golden gleam
Life, what is it but a dream?

Through The Looking-glass
Lewis Carroll

CONTENTS

INTRODUCTION

The stories in *Razzle Dazzle* are accounts of the time I spent
growing up in Hobart and Melbourne. When I began writing
these stories I found that the past is never really past. It is ever-
changing in the light of the new knowledge I acquire as I
remember. I used to think of my childhood as a jigsaw puzzle
with some of the pieces missing, but I now realise that is too
static an image. The past is more like a kaleidoscope with its
colourful, ever-changing patterns that are like flowers, like fire
crackers, like snow crystals, all dissolving and re-forming at the
turn of the cylinder.

They change just as our past changes. Recently a scrap of
the past changed for me forever. One of the images fixed in my
mind as long as I can remember, is an imagined picture of my
father as a small boy of seven, riding on the 'rassle-dassle' at
the Intercolonial Exhibition in Hobart in 1894. This picture is
strong because I have a letter my father wrote about the
'rassle-dassle'. The letter seems as fresh today as when he
penned it laboriously to his 'darling Uncle Wilfred'.

Because his father, also Arthur Leslie, died after a fall
from a horse before his son was born, Uncle Wilfred is
obviously an important male figure in the life of a little boy
who was brought up by a sorrowing widowed mother and a
strong matriarchal grandmother.

Somebody once told me that a razzle dazzle was the
original name for a merry-go-round, so I imagined this little
boy, wearing a green velvet suit, sitting on a painted horse,
going round and round and up and down, the way horses slide
up and down their poles on a superior merry-go-round. But
recently my publisher sent me a 1908 photograph by Harold
Cazneaux of a real razzle dazzle. And, click, the kaleidoscope
turned, the pattern changed. The razzle dazzle, marvellously

caught in this photograph so that movement and gaiety are suspended there, is nothing like the small merry-go-round of my imagination.

Cancel the shiny white horse, spotted with black, with its flaring nostrils and flowing mane. Substitute instead a large steel construction, with a central pole and struts to hold the seats. The old sepia photograph and my long-time image of the merry-go-round must merge.

The boy with the long golden ringlets blowing in the wind is now on a long seat, holding tightly to the steel struts.

He is flying through the air. He is flying.

Moira Watson
1990

RASSLE-DASSLE

My darling Uncle Wilfred
   are you quite well
I hope you are.
   Grandmama Giblin gave me
a lovely big book it is such
a lovely one, it has such a lot
about different kinds of
fish and it is called chatter-box
and there are such a lot of pages I am getting on with school
allright I like it and Sister
said after christmas holidays she
thinks I will go
into the next class higher than
the one I am in now.
   Have you heard anything
about the Exhibition here
they is the littlest train in
the world in the Exhibition
The Exhibition is so big outside and inside and
they is a rassle-dassle in the
Exhibition it is a thing
like a round-about only
it goes round and as it
goes round it goes up and then
down and it keeps on like

1

that and it is threepence
to go round for quarter
of a hour and it is threepence to go round five times
in the little train and I
have been on them both the
little train is the nicest
it has been open a week
and a half.

Mother teaches us songs
and I no Mrs henry
hawkins and Wot cher
and lots of others and I
can play a few duets to
and mother said that
she might put me into the
choir mother sends her love
to you and so do I
Good bye darling Uncle
Wilfred from Arthur Giblin

THE LOST FATHER

I have a day book or journal written by my grandfather Arthur Giblin in 1881, which contains tissue-thin ink copies of letters he has written to clients, and accounts he has rendered. But, every now and then amongst them, there is a copy of a personal letter, which I, and my father before me, read several times, deciphering the rather blotted writing, so that we could gain more knowledge of the man who was his father, my grandfather.

It is a sad voyage of discovery in a way, because he was obviously a man who loved children and animals, and was close to them.

Reading a letter like the one I have copied out below makes me realise what a loss he was to my father's boyhood; what an amount of simple goodness and closeness to nature he would have contributed to his children.

> Fernleigh,
> Hobart,
> 14th April 1881.

My dear Wilfred,

I was very pleased when I got home from dinner today to find a note waiting for me from my little brother over the Straits. I expect it must have taken you a long time to write it. It is fun in Melbourne, is it? I wish I was only over there with you for you know we would get Maria and go in the direction of the Royal Park, and call at a little shop on the left hand side on the way, and get one of Mr Guest's nice pound cakes, and then we would go to the Park, see all the animals, lions, tigers, leopards bears and have our lunch and go home after having enjoyed a good days outing — Ask

3

Maria to take you as she did me more than five years ago.

I had given me today two capital little bronze-wing pigeons, all feathered, such pretty birds, I must get you to feed them and look after them when you come back. Scamp and pup are getting on very well, but pup still keeps very thin. The other day Mrs Davies' man came over with a magpie and wanted to know if was ours, I did not think so as it is much cleaner and white and does not sing the same way. Burt however thought it was the same so we have kept it at any rate for the present.

I hope you are a good boy and don't give your mother any trouble. I think you are most lucky. I often see poor Artie at 9 o'clock tramping up to school, while you are enjoying yourself in Melbourne. Goodbye old fellow and mind you enjoy yourself thoroughly,

Your affectionate brother Arthur.

BLUE EYES — BEAUTY

My father asked me if I felt cold, but I said no, although I was just on the edge of being too cold. I was three years old, and I was going with my father to visit my mother in hospital, and to see my new baby sister. We lived at Bellerive, before the first bridge was built, so we travelled across to Hobart on the ferry. It was December, and we sat upstairs on the top deck. I don't think I had ever been on the ferry before, because I remember how delighted I was with the sunlight bouncing off the waves in little gleaming sparks.

I was three years old, and this was the most important thing that had happened in my life so far, so this first memory is quite strong. My father had a tweed hat on, and some sort of rough tweed jacket with leather buttons. I kept hold of one of the buttons on his sleeve, and traced the swirled pattern stamped into it with my finger.

I had a present for the baby wrapped up in pink paper — pink was for girls. We hadn't been able to find a piece of ribbon to put around it, so my father had fastened the end of the paper with a tiny piece of pink sticking plaster from the surgery. I thought it looked fine. It was before the days when you bought elaborate bows and cards to dress up gifts.

I can no longer remember what the present was. I know I chose it myself, and it was made of bright pink celluloid, but I don't know whether it was a duck for the bath or perhaps one of those kewpie dolls with a twirl of gold hair painted on top. I had a kewpie doll myself, its round eyes open in perpetual surprise, both its legs made in one piece so that it could stand up. I imagined my new sister and I playing together with twin kewpie dolls, but I don't know whether this was what I finally chose in the

5

shop. I have a brief memory of taking a long time to choose it, so you would think I would remember what it was.

My father said he would buy me an ice cream cone when we arrived in Hobart, and I sat and looked forward to this, imagining the thick, creamy taste of the yellow ice cream, and the lovely little pieces of salty ice in it.

I was in a state of bliss. I could only come down — and I did. When we got to the hospital, my mother was in bed, which was a shock. She didn't look sick though, and she was wearing her beautiful pink bed jacket which had swansdown around the neck and the wide sleeves.

The baby was tucked up in a small bassinet near her bed, sound asleep with just the top of her head and the tip of her nose showing outside her cocooning bunny-rug.

My mother said she was nearly due to be fed, so my father immediately picked her up. I kissed the top of her head, which smelt of talcum powder. Her hair was very straight and fair, and she had eyes of a dark yet milky blue. She didn't smile yet, and she didn't seem interested in me at all.

My parents talked about her. My father said she was a beautiful baby. My mother said she thought she was going to have blue eyes like my father. She said that all babies had these dark blue eyes at first, but that some changed later.

'Like yours, darling,' she added. 'Yours changed to hazel. A lovely colour.'

Her silver mirror was on a little table, so I looked at myself in it. I had eyes like pale green gooseberries, I realised. They even had flecks of brown in them, like ripe gooseberries get on their skins. I asked if there was any chance that they would still change to blue. My father said no, not at this stage, but repeated tactfully that they were a lovely colour.

The matron, large and jolly, came in and offered to show us the children's ward, perhaps because my father was a doctor. In one cot there was a little boy standing up, lonely and eager for attention. He threw his rabbit out on the floor, and laughed when I gave it back, and immediately threw it out again. I badly wanted to take him home.

'Would you like to change him for your baby?' asked the matron in her loud, jolly voice, and I nodded yes. I was embarrassed and upset when she burst out laughing. It was only a joke.

'I don't think we'll tell Mummy you wanted to exchange babies,' said my father when we went back to say goodbye to her. 'Our Bubba is really the best, you know. It won't be long before you'll be able to play with her.'

On the way home, while we waited for the ferry we bought a chocolate from the machine on the wharf. You put a penny in the slot, and a Nestlés chocolate in a red wrapper slid out when you pulled the handle.

It was cold going home, so we had to sit in the cabin, which smelt oily and horrible. I ate my penny chocolate, and then felt rather sick.

When I got home I had my bath. Joyce, the maid, dried me, and I sprinkled a lot of talcum powder on myself. The scent of it reminded me of my new baby. Although I didn't like Joyce much, because she hardly ever bothered to answer when I talked to her, I started to tell her about the baby. I told her about Bubba's blue eyes, and I even told her I wished my green ones would change colour, because they were like gooseberries.

'Ha!' said Joyce. She tied my dressing-gown too tightly.

'Green eyes — gooseberry pies,

Blue eyes — beauty,' she chanted.

You can see why I didn't like her.

After my little sister Bubba and I moved to Hobart, we had our photographs taken by a studio photographer. I can remember it well. I was four or five at the time. The photographer hid his head under a black cloth, which covered the back of the camera. He had long thin legs clad in black trousers, and it looked as if the camera had six legs.

'Now keep verrrry still,' he told us. Bubba was only a baby, and soon got tired of keeping still, so the photographer took some of me alone.

'Think about fairies,' he told me. 'Can you see lots of fairies

7

flying up there behind the camera?'

I could. I truly thought I could. I believed in fairies for years, having been brought up on the poetry of Robert Louis Stevenson. I was the child who clapped loudest and longest to save the fairy Tinkerbell when I went to the pantomime of Peter Pan at the Theatre Royal.

The photographer arranged to have one of the photographs of me published in the weekly magazine in Hobart. 'Tasmanian Childhood'. it said across the top. It was tinted a sort of apricot colour, so that you couldn't tell I had pale gold hair and green eyes. I was pleased about this, because I had hated my eyes ever since my sister had been born with dark blue eyes, which my parents hoped wouldn't change as she grew older.

I was a conceited little girl I imagine, and precocious too, always ready to recite Edward Lear's poetry for visitors who came to tea. I was proud of my big photograph from the Tasmanian Mail which stood on the mantelpiece, and I studied it whenever I went into the sitting room. I felt an empathy with it, that feeling that a photograph can induce if it seems to have captured one's essence.

My expression was compounded of a faint smugness — (I'm having more photos taken than you, Bubba, even if you have got blue eyes) — a slight surprise as if those fairies really were floating around just beyond the camera, and also a trace of sadness. As if I had a realisation already that life is fleeting; there was a photograph that haunted me of my baby brother's lonely grave, aged six days; and the memory of a white Persian kitten lying still with a bright ribbon of blood coming out of its mouth after the nursery fender fell on it.

I was proud of my own photograph, but only for a week or two. One afternoon I was lying on the floor in the sitting room, setting out my mother's mahjong tiles, which fascinated me. There were beautiful pictures of birds and flowers, of bamboos and strange Chinese characters etched on them in blue and green and red. The ivory felt very smooth, and slightly warm to the touch. I didn't know then about all the elephants who died to make the tiles for the ladies in Hobart to play with on green baize cloths. The box the tiles were kept in was made of sandalwood, and even now, if I go into a Chinese store and open one of those carved sandalwood chests which used, in my day, to be called glory boxes, the musty scent takes me back to that sitting room in Hobart, with its royal blue and pink Chinese carpet, and its black lacquer screen with inlaid birds. It was because of the screen that my parents didn't realise I was there, in the corner of the room.

'I don't like that photograph of Moira any more,' my mother said. 'Who could possibly hate me enough to write a thing like that about a little child? An anonymous letter's such a vicious thing.'

She sounded very upset.

'Hate's too strong a word, Rita,' said my father. He sounded upset too, but he was trying to soothe my mother. 'It was probably someone who was jealous because she would have liked to have her child's photo in the *Mail*.'

That was all they said. What did it mean? What terrible thing had this person said about me? I couldn't make myself ask, and I finished putting the tiles back in the box, and crept quietly out of the room.

I felt very badly about this thing I had overheard, and I worried about it for years, then it got buried in my subconscious mind until I was grown-up. One day I happened to glance at the photograph on the mantelpiece, and I asked, at last: 'By the way, Mum, what did the anonymous letter say about me? After that photograph was published?'

'Oh, didn't I ever tell you? It was terrible,' said my mother. 'I received a letter in the post saying "You think you're smart getting your little girl's photo in the paper, but you might notice the child's parting is crooked."'

It was such an anti-climax after all these years, that I looked blank.

'But, is that *all*?' I asked. 'I thought it was something awful.'

'But it is awful. Don't you see? It took all the joy out of a beautiful photograph. Every time I looked at it after that, all I noticed was your parting, and I remembered the horrible letter.'

All those years later, she still sounded upset. I studied the photograph. I had curly hair, but the crown of my head was smooth, so you could clearly see that careless zigzag of a parting.

I found a framed copy of that photograph in a drawer the other day, and I realised my mother had been right.

When I looked at the child in the photograph, all my eyes focused on was that small criss-cross of a parting, and all that I could feel was the pain inside my mother when she said: 'Who could possibly hate me enough to write a thing like that about a little child?'

LIFE WAS BUT A DREAM

For the first nine years of my life I lived in Hobart. My father was a doctor, and my mother went out quite a lot, playing bridge and mahjong and acting in plays put on by the local repertory company. I can remember her pacing the floor as she rehearsed her lines for *Riders to the Sea*. She had encouraged the company to stage it, being Irish and able to adopt a strong accent so easily.

I had a governess, shared with little sister Bubba as she grew old enough, a part-time Nanny, and there was a maid called Joyce who taught me fancy work and lent me a wonderful magazine called *Peg's Paper*, having sworn me, under fear of death, to keep it hidden from my mother.

Sometimes in the late afternoons my parents went to *thé dansants*, or invited friends around to listen to records on the gramophone they had imported from Melbourne. Tunes like 'The Desert Song' and 'The Red Shadow' floated upstairs to my bedroom, and I would climb out of bed and sit halfway down the stairs so that I could watch the grown-ups dancing in the study below. If I sat just above the bend in the stairs I could look down through the banisters, and nobody noticed me in the shadows.

Sometimes I was taken to parties where there were mainly grown-ups — a crayfish picnic down at Brown's River when the Royal Navy was in port, or to tennis at Government House, or afternoon tea, which was a bit boring. I must have been a precocious little girl, because I was taught long poems by my governess and my mother, and stood up quite happily in front of the adults and recited 'The Owl and the Pussy Cat' or 'The New Vestments'. The latter poem of Lear's was always a great success, although I thought it was extremely rude. It was about an old man whose clothes were all made of vegetables, which were demolished by various animals.

'And so he ran home with no clothes on at all!' I would end with a rush in my precise little English voice, feeling my cheeks growing pink.

I have a memory of reciting thus between the grown-ups' sets of tennis at Government House, and the Governor's daughter giving me a tennis ball, which was, I considered, quite a prize.

One birthday my parents decided to give me a party at the Hobart Zoo. I do not, you notice, say *which* birthday. I would have liked to state 'my parents gave me a party at the zoo on my fifth birthday'. But was it my fifth or my sixth, or perhaps, as I seem to remember so little about the details, was it only my fourth birthday?

I always have this trouble with my early childhood in Hobart. It is dateless, timeless, and I seemed to have no idea of the passing of the years, to have kept no track of events in chronological order. It wasn't until I came over to Melbourne when I was nine and attended a real school, with the year neatly divided into terms, that I realised why my early life had been unsegmented. There was nothing to sharpen the hazy days — no school uniforms to acquire, no pile of exciting new school books with their smell of fresh print to feast on all at once. No speculations about which teacher I would have, which friends would be in my class. No school holidays to punctuate the year when schoolwork began to pall.

I was certainly not unhappy with either of my governesses. I can still remember being richly entertained by being taught to read at an early age, and consuming all of Dickens, and discussing poetry. I can't remember doing much arithmetic, but I did start to learn French.

Life certainly wasn't quite real. My father played the piano and taught me songs.

> *Merrily merrily merrily merrily,*
> *Life is but a dream,*

I sang, and was closer to the truth than I knew.

12

This birthday party at the Hobart Zoo is an example.

The more I try to remember the party, the more dreamlike it seems.

I *know* it happened. I just wish I remembered more of the details. It's rather like having the jigsaw puzzle with some of the pieces missing, but in this case it's the main pieces that are missing and all the boring sky is filled in.

I can remember my mother cutting up pink and blue crepe paper into squares, and placing a handful of peanuts in the centre of each square, and my father tied each one with ribbon to make a little bundle for each child to feed the monkeys.

I can remember too that there was trouble about the balloons — they couldn't be blown up until we got to the zoo, but who was suddenly going to blow up forty balloons? I don't know what the solution was, but balloons there certainly were, straining against a rather grey and windy sky.

That was another thing I can recall — the worry about the weather. It was overcast in the morning. What if it poured?

This worry was overcome when Margaret O'Grady, the Governor's daughter, rang my mother to say that if it rained we could all come over to Government House and play in the ballroom. It would have been very handy, because it was just across the Domain, close to the zoo.

I prayed hard that it wouldn't rain because I was looking forward immensely to seeing how pleased the rabbits were when forty children fed them with pieces of bread. There were so many rabbits that they hardly ever all got a turn. I think that Nanny would have quite liked it to rain. She said there would be one or two parents who would have been pleased if their children had ended up at Government House.

And now I can see one of the problems of writing about my childhood. A kind of reverse snobbery. It sounds as if you're skiting when you talk about nannies (even if they're only shared) and it's boring to talk about Government House. I would much prefer to have some down-to-earth memories of a childhood spent in the bush, in some extreme of poverty perhaps, so that I had grown up close to nature and elemental things. I was one remove from real life a lot of the time, except in the garden, which I loved.

The garden at King Street, Sandy Bay, is real to me still. I could take you right around that garden, past the green globules on the gooseberry canes, and the crimson splashes of raspberries on the brick paths. There was an old apple tree in one corner — Cox's Orange Pippin. Who could forget such a name? It was quite a small apple, but to bite into one was as intoxicating as my first glass of wine years later.

Near that was the fowlyard. In those days my father, who had a fondness for chooks dating back to his childhood, was allowed to keep his six white Leghorns and six Buff Orpingtons right up against our neighbour's fence. Sometimes when a hen went broody, my father bought it a clutch of eggs, and then I used to pray we wouldn't have a thunderstorm to prevent the chickens hatching out.

Next came the best part of the garden — a long white pergola, thickly covered with a gnarled wistaria. My swing hung from one of the cross beams, and when the wistaria was flowering for all too brief a time, the mauve blossoms hung down against the blue of the sky like bunches of pale grapes, or drifted down on me as I swung. Their perfume hung all around, so heady that, combined with the swinging, I used to become quite dizzy. When my father came out in the garden once, I stopped swinging to tell him how beautiful it all was, and realised I felt very strange.

'Are you all right, darling? You're a bit pale,' he said.

'No, I'm going to be sick,' I said, and was. After that, whenever grown-ups were around, they kept telling me not to swing for too long.

The swing had such long chains on it that I could work myself up to see right over the back fence. Sometimes if nobody stopped me I could keep going long enough and high enough to make the swing go slightly crooked and out of control, which was scary but exciting too. When I could see over the wall like the child in the poem, what I hoped to catch a glimpse of was a double-decker tram going past, although the best view of these was from my upstairs corner window. It was one of my favourite occupations indoors, hearing the *rackety rack* of a tram approaching down the hill, then watching it rocking around our corner on its silver tracks, a wonderful green double-decker tram, with the people who had been brave enough to climb upstairs almost on a level with my eyes.

I studied their faces as they swayed past, and wondered if they felt as I did, that one day perhaps the tram would tip over as it turned the corner. I had a secret desire that this would happen, so that I felt half terrified, half excited each time a tram went past. I didn't envisage the people getting hurt — no blood — I hated the thought of blood. I just imagined them climbing out of the upstairs windows, shaking their heads sadly at the tram lying flat on its side. I didn't envisage any damage to the tram either — I dearly loved those double-decker trams, but I obviously craved a little more drama in my life.

Although there was a tram stop quite close to our front gate, we hardly ever went on a tram. When we went out, it was for walks with Bubba in the pram. There was a small and lovely park only a short distance away, where we could make daisy chains, and in the other direction we could walk down towards the sea at Sandy Bay. No need for a tram ride.

And, to tell the truth, when I did occasionally go into the city on a tram, I found it a bit disappointing. Once you were inside the tram, it seemed much safer, hardly an adventure at all. I felt foolish to think I had imagined it was really going to fall over, as it ploughed steadily along the tracks towards its destination.

It was one more proof to me that life was more exciting in my imagination than in the real world.

Moira with Teddy in the vegetable garden, Hobart, 1926.

MAMA DOLL

When I was five I caught pneumonia. I must have been very ill, because whenever I woke up my mother or father were sitting in a chair by my bed, even if it was the middle of the night. My mother kept sponging me with a new yellow sponge to cool me down. My father took my temperature a lot, and tried to make me have sips of lemon barley water.

Once my mother went out of the room for a minute, and Joyce came and stood in the doorway. There was somebody else standing behind her, but I couldn't see who it was.

'She's very bad. She's got *double* pneumonia,' Joyce said in a loud voice. Joyce couldn't have talked softly if her life depended upon it. I closed my eyes because I didn't want Joyce to come in and talk to me. The words kept echoing around the room, bouncing off the walls and making my head ache. '*Double* pneumonia, *double* pneumonia…'

My mother came back with a fresh jug of barley water.

'Hush, Joyce,' she said. 'Please don't disturb her.'

'It's *double* pneumonia,' I told my mother.

It seemed to take me a long while to get better. I couldn't be bothered with anything. I even got tired of people reading to me.

One day my mother asked my father if he would be there for a while, because she wanted to go out and buy me a present. I wasn't very interested in the thought of a present — I had been given lots of presents while I was ill — but this one was different. My mother came back and laid a doll beside me. She was made of china, and had blue eyes that opened and closed. I had never seen a doll that went to sleep before. I was enthralled, absolutely delighted. I sat her up and laid her down until my arms were tired.

17

'There's another thing she does,' said my mother, and bent her forward.

Immediately a tiny 'Ma ma' came tremblingly from her chest. It was magic. I tenderly stroked her perfect pink hands, then I decided to take off her bootees to look at her feet — and discovered that her body was made of calico. She had a stuffed calico body! For a moment my joy was diminished, but somehow I suddenly felt more maternal towards her. She was so vulnerable, she could be so easily destroyed if Rover, our dog, got hold of her, for instance. When I pulled down her long pink and white dress, nobody could tell about her white cloth body. It was our secret.

I suddenly wanted to get better quickly so that I could wheel her around in my doll's pram. I ate all my meals, and when it was time to have my Robeline I asked if I could have a second spoonful to help me to get strong more quickly. Robeline had the most delicious flavour, like melted toffee, so it was lucky it was so good for you. I loved the jar it was in too. I can remember that, but not what the picture on the jar was actually like. I became terribly spoilt at this stage I am sure. People still kept giving me presents. The darling elderly man who lived opposite sent things across for me. He had a chauffeur called Horricks or Horlicks — something like that — I know it reminded me of malted milk. I was in love with Horricks, who had a lovely dark green uniform and shiny leggings and a peaked cap. I hoped that he wouldn't get married so that I could marry him when I grew up. Horricks brought over bags of walnuts from the big trees in their garden, and huge dark cherries. I tried to keep two pairs of cherries to wear over my ears for ear rings, but I always ended up eating them. I was pleased when Horricks was sent over to ask how I was getting on, but a bit disappointed that he didn't bother to wear his peaked cap.

Life returned to its old routine. My parents played the gramophone again. It seemed ages since I had heard the Riffs' Song. I sat on the stairs nursing my mama doll, and watched the grown ups dancing. Every now and again I made my doll, who was called Betty, go to sleep. I noticed her eyes seemed to be sticking a bit, so I tried to help her to close them, and suddenly they disappeared inside her head. I was filled with horror. She seemed so real to me that it was as if I had killed her.

I stumbled down the stairs, awash with tears, causing consternation among the grown-ups. My poor parents, they didn't entertain their friends very often, and I always seemed to manage to upset things. I wonder if perhaps I did it on purpose to gain their attention. The Riffs' Song was turned off in mid 'Ho', and I tried to explain what had happened.

My father realised that this was a major tragedy for me, and he said comfortingly: 'Come on, I'm sure I can fix her. We'll go into the study and find something among my instruments to hook her eyes back again.'

Never has a loving mother hovered more anxiously over an injured child. She looked so terrible with those two gaping holes in her head that it was hard to believe how much like a real baby she had seemed a short time ago. It was harder to fix her than my father had thought it would be. He tried various instruments, and then my mother's button hook. My mother suggested that perhaps she would have to go to the dolls' hospital, which caused another flood of tears.

Joyce came in just then, to say my bath was ready, so my father said he would bring Betty up when I was in bed.

I was having a bath with Bubba and going to bed early since I had been ill. I quite liked having my bath with Bubba, because we played with ducks or boats, which would have seemed a bit babyish if I had been in the bath alone. The thing we both wanted at the same time though, was the new sponge.

We had lovely sponges in Hobart, real yellow sea sponges with lots of holes where the sea creatures had swum in and out. Today, if you ask for a sponge at the chemist's they are likely to try to sell you a horrible oblong of plastic. Bubba and I fought over the sponge in the bath. Bubba liked to suck it. I used to ask her firmly if she had wee'd in the bath, because it wouldn't have been hygienic to drink the bathwater if she had. Bubba would shake her head, and go on sucking the sponge.

'Hygienic' was a word we learnt very early in life, because our father was keen on it. Washing our hands, and not eating things we had dropped on the floor, and all that sort of thing.

I can remember that there was a blowfly buzzing around a plate of sliced Stras sausage at the tuckshop of the first school we went to later in Melbourne. I thought I was being helpful when I said to the lady: 'Excuse me, but there's a fly on the food and it isn't very hygienic.' I can still remember the awful look she gave me.

We had a clay bubble pipe in the bath on the night my father was fixing up Betty's eyes. You rubbed soap around the edge of the bowl of the pipe, and then blew. Bubba blew too hard, so the bubbles wouldn't come, which made her very upset. I played a game where she held out her hands, and I carefully blew a bubble into them, then she clapped her hands together and burst it. She had fat pink baby hands, all wrinkled from being in the water. Each time she burst a bubble she couldn't stop laughing. I realised I had missed her very much while I was sick. At the back of my mind though, I was worrying about Betty.

My father brought her up when I was having my tea in bed.

'I'm afraid she had to have quite an operation, but her eyes are fixed,' he said. I could see what he meant when I changed her into her nightie later. He had had to take her head off, where it joined her calico body, and he had stuck it on again with lots of sticking plaster.

I think he was a bit worried about her operation. When he came up to kiss me goodnight he asked if I had looked at her neck.

He said he was sorry if it looked a bit of a mess.

'It was one of the hardest operations I have ever had to perform,' he said, and I felt quite proud that Betty had got all that attention.

MY DARLING KIDDO

My mother's most treasured possession was a pillowcase.
Yellowed with age, and beginning to disintegrate, it was stuffed
full of love letters. Letters written to her by my father when they
met in the Middle East in 1917, when she was a Queen
Alexandra Nursing Sister, and he was a Captain in the Royal
Army Medical Corps.

There must have been over a hundred of these letters, but
when I said to my father that they must have been separated for
a lot of the time after they first met, he looked surprised. He
replied Not at all, only when he was assigned for short stretches
of duty at other camps. The truth was, he was a very romantic
man, and a prolific letter writer, and he sent my mother two or
even three letters a day when he was away from her.

My parents were married at the Consulate in Cairo in 1919,
and came back to Melbourne. When they went to collect my
mother's cabin trunks from the wharf, all her belongings had been
stolen. Wedding presents, clothes, family photographs in heavy
silver frames ('If only they had left me the photos,' she mourned
over the years). Nothing remained of her early life in Longford,
Ireland. Nothing remained but the lumpy pillowcase. Sometimes
my mother mourned in a keening Irish fashion (that is the only
way I can describe it) for her lost family mementoes, but she
always ended up by saying at least the thieves had been kind
enough to leave her the letters. My sister and I thought that it was
less kindness that had motivated them than a realisation that the
letters were of no material use to them at all. Even the pillowcase
itself, although made of fine Irish linen, and hand-embroidered,
was stained and rather worn after its travels through various army
camps in the Middle East.

My younger sister and I were fascinated by this long corre-
spondence, probably because we realised how much my mother
treasured it.

When we left Hobart when I was nine to make our home in
Melbourne, all sorts of possessions were given away or thrown
out. In fact I became rather alarmed as old books and toys and
shabby but familiar pieces of furniture were jettisoned... but
never the letters in their unromantic receptacle.

I forgot about the letters for years when I married and left
home, until the time came, inevitably, when, both my parents
having died, my sister and I were sorting out the contents of the
family home before the auction. There, on top of our mother's
wardrobe, was the disintegrating pillowcase. The contents spilled
out onto the floor through rents in the linen as I took it down. We
settled down on the faded purple and grey carpet to examine
them. Dozens and dozens of cheap army envelopes, grey to match
the shabby carpet and the coldness of the house. Postmarked
blackly, and passed by the censor. Although he had presumably
read them, we were curiously loath to do so, but eventually we
each took one out of its envelope. It was almost as if we said 'I
dare you' to each other.

'My darling Kiddo,' mine started off, in my father's thin
distinctive writing.

'I am writing two letters today my own sweet little love,
because although it is only an hour since you left, I am so lonely
without you, and thinking of you on that long, hot trip back to
Buelah, and hoping Matron didn't put you straight on night
duty...'

Or words to that effect. It was at about this stage that I
paused and said to my sister that I thought these letters were very
private, and I wondered if we should read them or not.

She replied that she felt the same way. What should we do
with them? With hindsight, perhaps we should have put them
back in the yellow pillowcase until we were feeling less emotional.

But on that morning, determined to empty out the surgery
papers, and anything else we felt should be destroyed, we had lit

22

Mother, (left), father, Sister Quin and Matron (on the camel) at the Pyramids, 1918.

Rita Flanagan, my mother, wearing Arthur's uniform at 48th Headquarters, Alexandria. Matron can't have been around.

the big incinerator in the back garden. It was lustily consuming twenty years or so of editions of the *British Medical Journal*, and its Australian counterparts, which had provided a cosy nest for silverfish in the window seat in the surgery, plus all the medical records which were more than seven years old, and numerous medical samples and desk diaries.

My sister and I gathered up the dusty pile of letters from the floor, took them outside and consigned them to the flames. Yet, even as the tongues of fire crackled over the bone-dry envelopes, and the smell of burnt cloth lingered in our nostrils, I was having regrets. The urge to follow up a story which had started me on an Arts degree with a view to becoming a journalist, made me hunger now for the details of the events, the times, the places of these heady and dangerous happenings.

But, most of all, I realised as time went by, they might have provided some clues to me about my mother, my warm-hearted, emotional yet will-o-the-wisp of a mother.

ANGEL'S FOOD

My mother died at the age of sixty-nine after a long, sad illness. She was seriously injured in a car accident, and had several blood transfusions. She became very jaundiced, and was progressively confused and agitated until her death two years later. She kept a tin beside her bed — a flat, rather battered tin with a picture of three sad-looking Persian kittens on the lid. It had originally contained Dutch confectionery of some sort, but during her final illness it was the repository for her most treasured possessions. It was her only concrete link with the past, and her security for the present, when most things were becoming too difficult for her to cope with.

It contained her wide gold wedding ring, now too tight for her arthritic finger, a postcard my father sent his mother for Christmas, 1916, from France, a love letter he sent my mother on 28th January, 1919, from Abbassia, and her wedding certificate, dated 14th June, 1919.

This wedding certificate was signed by the British Consul, who had married them 'according to the provisions of the Foreign Marriage Act of 1892', and the ceremony took place in Cairo. The certificate cost my father three shillings and sixpence. It was a fitting ending to a strange, exotic courtship, alternating between long, arduous stretches on theatre duty, and dreamlike idylls of off-duty outings. The fading photographs show 'Rita in the Garden of Gethsemane', 'Rita and I at the Pyramids' (on camels) and 'Rita on the Lake of Galilee' — in a boat, looking dreamy and enigmatic. Matron figures in a number of these photos. My father told us that she chaperoned her nurses very conscientiously, which is perhaps why my parents took to the lake to escape.

The sepia postcard in my mother's cat tin was written by my father at what must have been the lowest point in his life. It has a depressing picture of a soldier in a trench at the Front, tin-helmeted, gun beside him, and thoughts of home and Christmas wreathing up from the smoke of a small brazier.

Inscribed 'Christmas Greetings 7th Division, 1916, Ypres, Neuve, Festubert, Givenchy, Loos, the Somme', it sends a far from cheery Christmas message from my father, normally the most optimistic of human beings. He wrote to his mother:

'...perhaps later on we may all get together again, though things seem to be going badly for us at present, with the Germans over-running Roumania, and Greece against us. However, it's a long lane that has no turning, so we'll hope for the best. Have been very busy today, and have seen over two hundred cases...'

Little did he know that he was shortly to contract Scarlet Fever, was actually sickening with it already, probably, which would add to his depression. He was invalided to Gaza to recover, to a more leisurely war and certainly a more romantic one with the arrival of my mother in his life.

He must have had some lighter moments in France too. My grandmother once gave my sister and me some postage stamps on old post-cards, including another one he sent from France.

It said he was going to be married, that she was blonde and English and her name was Ruby.

'Ruby!' chorused my sister and I, round-eyed with amazement.

'Were you engaged when you met mummy?'

'Well, yes,' admitted our father, brushing his hand over his head as he always did if he felt a bit sheepish about something. 'But once I met Rita — your mother — of course...'

Our mother, not to be outdone, said airily: 'I was engaged, too.'

We were shocked. 'He was engaged to both of you?'

'No, no. I was engaged to a banker back in Ireland. But, once I met your father, of course...'

26

We were enthralled by the fragments of these heady war-torn times that were occasionally brought to light.

'Tell us about your wedding reception again.'

It was our favourite story. My mother, a natural actress, would launch forth without further prompting. Their wedding reception had been a luncheon at the elegant Shepheard's Hotel, which made the incident that occurred more hilarious to us.

After the main courses, my parents had decided on Angel's Food for dessert. This was an orange and lemon concoction, with clear jelly on top of a mousse base. It was still popular in my childhood. On this occasion, the waiter, bearing the dessert triumphantly aloft on a silver tray, collided with another waiter coming out the swing door of the kitchen. My mother happened to be watching, as the first waiter, undaunted, scooped it back onto the tray, spat on his brown hands, and smoothed it back into shape. He then placed it on the centre of the wedding breakfast table. After all, food was very short at the end of the war, and to waste it would have been a crime. My mother, torn between demanding that it be taken back to the kitchen, and a dislike of causing a scene at her wedding, compromised by telling my father in an urgent whisper not to eat any.

As a child, when we had Sunday midday dinner with our parents, we sometimes had Angel's Food after the roast dinner. I was never fond of it. I can still remember looking at it, glistening in a cut-crystal bowl, and visualising the shiny globules of spit on that long-ago Angel's Food. I would say I wasn't hungry any longer, and after a while my mother took the hint, and we then had chocolate blancmange every week instead.

I still have the battered tin with the sad kittens painted on the lid, and my mother's treasures inside it. I know she would want me to keep them safe.

Moira with Rita, Hobart, 1923.

IT CREPT BACK IN

My mother had cut Ireland out of her heart, but obstinately it crept back in. It became a shadowy background to my childhood.

My mother used certain words and phrases which other people in Hobart did not use.

I was often 'alanna' — Irish for 'darling'. Our dog was a lovely 'tosie'. If something annoyed my mother, she was apt to say 'musha!' which she said meant 'bother'.

Ireland crept in too, in a more concrete form, with letters bearing stamps with a map of Eire. Letters from my Aunt Kitty, whom I had never seen, who was also, puzzlingly, 'Mary, Blessed Bride of Oliver Plunkett'. I asked my governess about Oliver Plunkett, and she looked him up in the encyclopaedia, and found that he lost his head. My mental pictures of Aunt Kitty's life were very muddled indeed.

My mother was the second of five children. Her mother died of tuberculosis when she was twelve and she went to live with her mother's relatives, the Sheridans of Castlebar, but Kitty, aged two, went to be looked after by the Sisters of Mercy.

I can remember my mother saying to my father: 'Kitty has gone into a closed order. I don't know — I think it is better to help people in a practical way, rather than pray for them.'

Poor Aunt Kitty, spending her days on her knees, praying for the sins of the world. Or lucky Aunt Kitty? Who knows?

My mother was the practical one, who became a Queen Alexandra Nursing Sister, and went to the First World War to save lives.

English lives. And there is another paradox. Longford, where her family lived, is up towards the north. Her father, a bank manager, and the three boys belonged to the Sinn Fein in the days when it wasn't such a crime to do so. I can remember being proud when I heard that my Uncle Joe had swum the River Liffey to escape from the Black and Tans, who were firing at him.

And all the while, Aunt Kitty stayed behind the walls of the Repatrix Convent in Limerick. She sent presents to Bubba and me, and this was puzzling too, because I wasn't allowed to wear the ivory cross that had been blessed by the Pope, or the beautiful blue beads.

'No, I'm sorry, you can't wear it, alanna, it's a rosary.'

It broke my heart when it was given to Mary, our maid, who was a member of the Catholic faith and thus deserving of it.

I was allowed to keep the little illuminated prayers, and a red heart made of shining material with blanket stitching around the edge. This was the Bleeding Heart of Jesus. I don't know what happened to it. I kept it in my drawer for years, wrapped up in a hanky. I had a strange sad feeling when I took it out and looked at it, but I didn't know why.

My mother could never bring herself to write and tell Aunt Kitty she was no longer a Catholic, so she had to live with this deception. She did it for Aunt Kitty's sake. She said she thought the news would kill her.

Even in her childhood, my mother had questioned the way the names of the parishioners who hadn't paid their tithes were read out in church.

'But they were so poor they couldn't even feed their children properly,' she told us, her eyes flashing all those years later.

She gradually stopped going to mass in Hobart. Nevertheless, I can remember when I was quite small that she was very upset the day the priest crossed the street to avoid speaking to her.

When I think of my father, I have a clear and instant picture in my mind. My mother is more elusive.

Warm-hearted and amusing, bright as a flitting butterfly, she was sometimes as sad as the shores of her tormented Ireland.

There was another side to my mother which intrigued us very much. Although she was intelligent and well-read, she occasionally came out with remarks that were worthy of an Irish joke.

We were so surprised and amused on these occasions that it

30

was hard not to laugh, but the good thing about my mother was that she always saw the joke and joined in too, laughing until she cried.

One day Bubba said to her: 'Mummy, excuse me but why do you always say "Ah, widdown," after you've laughed?'

'What? What do you mean, Bubba? I've never said "widdown" in my life.' My mother sounded quite taken aback, and she repeated 'widdown, widdown', several times half under her breath, as if testing the word out on her tongue.

Bubba could be obstinate. 'Yes, you do,' she persisted. 'When you've really laughed a lot. Like the "No conveniences"...'

This was one of our favourite jokes about our Mother. One Sunday we had gone for a picnic lunch at Seaford, quite an outing in about 1933, past small seaside towns like Mordialloc and Edithvale and Carrum (maybe not in that order). Seaford in the 1930s seemed an exciting destination. Several hundred yards of tea-tree scrub to cross, and then we reached the small sandhills which protected us from the wind, if it happened to be blowing. We could venture over the top to see the long stretch of firm beach where we could run and draw with sticks and make sand-castles, and beyond that was the blue sprawl of the sea, enticing yet slightly frightening. (In Hobart we had been to Sandy Bay beach and Brown's River rarely. It was always too cold, we were told.)

It was on our way back from one of these rare Sunday picnics at Seaford that my mother made one of her Irish jokes.

She stopped on the sandy track, beside a small wooden notice which pointed down a bisecting track.

'Will you look at that,' she said. 'What a strange notice to put up: "No Conveniences".'

The rest of the family were silent for a moment, disbelieving our ears. Even Bubba could spell by now, and she caught my eye and we were helpless.

My father said: 'If you put your glasses on, my love, I think you will find it says "To Conveniences".'

'Of course, of course,' said my mother, and she laughed too, laughed until tears ran down her face and she had to wipe her eyes.

Now, five years later, Bubba enticed this story from our parents again. We both remembered it perfectly well, Bubba and I, but I think we felt it cheered our parents up to tell it again. We all laughed and felt safe and jolly and invulnerable. We felt like the adults, Bubba and I, when we played these little charades, and we gave each other meaningful looks.

Our parents acted their parts too, and spoke the right words, made the right gestures, and we all laughed far longer than the joke warranted.

'Ah,' said my mother, wiping her eyes with her handkerchief. 'Ah, widdown!'

MAGENTA

I didn't go to school when I lived in Hobart. I had governesses until we came to live on the mainland. When I was about six I had a governess called Miss Crane. I shared her with three friends of about my own age, and we sat around a large table in the nursery to do our lessons.

Miss Crane must have been a natural teacher, because we thoroughly enjoyed ourselves. Perhaps this was because Miss Crane had obviously majored in English and history, and our studies were heavily biased in that direction, at the expense of arithmetic and geography, both of which I found very boring.

The only disturbing element was my little sister Bubba, three years old at this time, only half our ages, yet forced to join us for lessons when my mother or the maid were too busy to look after her. Poor Bubba, how boring it must have been for her copying out rows of pot-hooks or colouring in endless pictures. It was no wonder she often disappeared under the long green baize cloth and distracted us by playing with our feet, pretending to be a naughty puppy under the table.

One evening my father came home and announced to my mother that he had some new patients who had arrived from the mainland. Their name was Van Ashe, and they were very concerned about schooling for their one little girl, Marie.

'In fact, Rita,' confessed my father, 'in a weak moment I suggested to them that Marie might be able to come and share Moira's lessons.'

'Musha!' said my mother. It was Irish for 'bother' and she only said it when she was very put out.

'Well, it would be a help with Miss Crane's salary,' pointed out my father. He supported a small army of retainers, so my mother agreed immediately, although I could sense she wasn't entirely happy.

The morning arrived when Mrs Van Ashe and Marie were to visit us, and I think we were all hating the idea, including Miss Crane. We had Bubba sharing our lessons that morning because my mother didn't trust Joyce, the maid, to make the scones for Mrs Van Ashe's morning tea.

Miss Crane had handed out maps of the world she had traced, and we were colouring in the British Empire in red crayon. At least, the others were using red, but I was using magenta. Magenta. I was obsessed with the name and the colour. Dark, rich and mysterious — reminiscent of the juice of the over-ripe raspberries that dropped from the canes and splattered their juice on the brick-paved paths of the vegetable garden. It even seemed to me to conjure up their special scent, redolent of summer. I had told Miss Crane how I felt about magenta and she looked it up in her encyclopaedia for me. She told me it came from a dye called fuchsine, and was called magenta because it was discovered in the year 1859, and named after the bloodshed at the battle of Magenta.

'This was the scene of the French–Sardinian victory over the Austrians, which occurred in the same year,' she told me. I wished in a way that she hadn't said this, because I hadn't associated the rich, reddish purple of magenta with blood before. That was the reason why I avoided using the bright red crayon in each new set of colours I was given. Red was the colour of horror, of blood, of death. It always made me think of the small fluffy white kitten I had been given, which one minute had been chasing a coloured ball across the floor, and the next had scrambled up the nursery firescreen, and had managed to pull it down on top of itself. Red was the colour of the blood which came out of its tiny mouth, staining its snowy fur. My father buried it under the wistaria creeper in the corner of the garden, and my mother told me it had gone to heaven. It was my first experience of death and heaven.

Anyway, we were all colouring in our maps assiduously the

morning Mrs Van Ashe was coming, taking care not to go over the edges into the ocean. It was a help that we had each been given a new box of waxy crayons, so the points weren't blunted yet. Bubba, as usual, was given all our old stubs to put in her blue pencil case. Poor Bubba, she never got a new box of crayons, because she would have broken them in a few minutes, but she never ceased to covet the new magenta crayon in each set I got, maybe because she knew how much I prized it.

There was a knock on the door, and mummy came in with a strange lady and a girl of about my age. The lady had a long black suit on, and a black hat with a long feather in it. She was the sort of person who wore a dead animal around her neck, with its tail in its mouth and glittering eyes, and this put me off her immediately. The girl had a brown velvet dress with rows and rows of lace, and one of those faces with hardly any mouth and no chin at all. She looked around the nursery with the sort of look which made it seem suddenly shabby, and she smiled in a secret, sneering way at my salmon pink teddy bear which had only one eye. Mummy was trying to match it up with a new one, but hadn't managed it yet.

My mother introduced Mrs Van Ashe and Marie to Miss Crane and to all of us, and explained that Marie might be coming to share our lessons. We made secret faces at each other to show how much we hated the idea, and Marie didn't look any keener than we did.

My mother realised that Bubba was missing, and she asked anxiously: 'Do you know where Bubba is, Miss Crane? I thought she was up here with you.'

Miss Crane turned rather pink and said quickly: 'She's under the table — er — looking for her pencil, Mrs Giblin.'

And then, right on cue, Bubba said loudly and clearly, even though she was under the tablecloth: 'Miss Crane, I can see your knickers. They're pink. Mummy, I can see Miss Crane's knickers. They're pink. Moi, I can see...'

Miss Crane was beautiful, with bobbed fair hair and grey eyes, but when she got upset she became rather red in the face. I

35

have never seen her as red as she got now, and she said in a really terrible voice: 'Bubba, come out from under the table at once.'

Sometimes Bubba didn't take any notice of Miss Crane, but this time she obeyed immediately, crawling out on all fours with her mouth open and her tongue lolling out like a puppy. Bubba was a pretty little girl with bright blue eyes like my mama doll, and pale golden hair, straight, with a fringe in front. Usually she looked plump and solemn and sweet, but today she had a tear in her smock, and looked almost neglected. She had a bit of fluff sticking to one eyebrow, and she stood up rubbing her bottom and looking reproachfully at Miss Crane. I think Miss Crane might have accidentally kicked her.

Bubba rolled her eyes in a funny way she had when we were playing games and she was pretending to be mad.

'Mummy,' she said, 'Miss Crane has pink knickers. Moi, did you know Miss Crane has pink knickers on? Mummy...'

'Yes, you've already told us that, alanna,' interrupted my mother, swooping on Bubba and giving her a big hug. 'Alanna' is Irish for 'darling' and my mother called us that when she was feeling especially fond of us.

'That's quite enough about Miss Crane's knickers, Bubba,' she continued in an amused sort of voice. 'Come on darling, show Mrs Van Ashe and Marie what you have been drawing this morning.'

I have never been prouder of my mother than I was at that moment. She sounded as if subjects like knickers were discussed every day in our house. She didn't look shocked at all, unlike Mrs Van Ashe, whose face was absolutely horrified, and who would obviously have liked to drag little Marie away from this contaminated atmosphere immediately. This of course was back in the days when ladies' underwear was never mentioned in public, let alone advertised on the radio. Who would have guessed that one day there would be a magic screen on which beautiful sexy girls would dance around in their skin-tight briefs singing: 'It's gotta be Bonds', or even worse, carelessly flick their skirts up, and say: 'Look, I'm wearing No Knickers.'

Poor Mrs Van Ashe. She was in a very unfortunate position. She certainly didn't want Marie to be tainted by the unhealthy atmosphere in our school room, but on the other hand, she didn't want to offend their new doctor and my mother, whom she had realised by now knew a lot of people the Van Ashes would like to meet in Hobart.

She had to put on a brave front, and try to sound enthusiastic.

'I hear you are an excellent teacher, Miss Crane. Now, what about French? Do you teach it? Marie started to learn French in Melbourne and I am most anxious for her to continue with it.'

'No, no French for another year at least, I am afraid, Mrs Van Ashe. Mrs Giblin and I consider that the girls are too young.'

Miss Crane had glanced at my mother as she spoke, and their faces both went carefully blank, the way grown-ups do when they are fibbing, which is a dead give-away. We all studiously avoided looking at the side table where there was a small pile of new text books with 'Le chat et le chien' on the cover.

'Oh well, in that case I'm afraid...' murmured Mrs Van Ashe with relief, and my mother, with her most gracious smile, said quickly: 'Well, that's a pity then, but I believe there is an excellent French teacher at the college, and no doubt Marie will be able to come and play with the girls after school some time.' Drawing a deep breath she added: 'And you and your husband must come to a small party we are having next month, Mrs Van Ashe. Now we will leave you to continue your lessons in peace, Miss Crane. Come on Bubba, you may come down and have morning tea with Marie.'

But Bubba wasn't quite ready to leave yet. Pulling away from my mother, she came to stand beside my chair. I had returned to colouring my map, which was finished except for the small — incredibly small — red dot that was Tasmania, the whole of my world. Bubba waited patiently until I had finished, her eyes glued to my new magenta crayon.

'Gimme, Moi,' she said firmly, holding out a small palm. Until this moment it hadn't occurred to me that she had actually planned the whole incident this morning. She was such a little girl, wasn't she? Little more than a baby really. It was surely just lucky coincidence that she had managed to shock Mrs Van Ashe. But as I watched the plump fingers close tightly over the magenta crayon like the pink petals of my mother's day-flowering cactus, I realised from the triumphant secret smile Bubba gave me that it was indeed payment for a job well done.

GIVE IT ROOM TO GROW

When I was about six, my father said I seemed to be fond of gardening, so would I like a garden of my own? He dug an oblong patch of soil for me, near the back fence, and I felt as if I had been given a present.

There wasn't much in it at first, except a Banksia rose, trained over a small archway. I loved it, and that was why I had chosen this particular part of the garden.

The earth was cold in Hobart in the winter. Most of my garden lay dormant. I cheated, and sifted gently through the topsoil with my finger tips, to see how soon the bulbs would come spearing through.

The snowdrops would be the first. When they flowered, their white bells told me that spring would be coming soon. The gardener who came when my father was too busy to do the garden moved three jonquil bulbs for me, and told me I would soon have a clump of them. Their heady perfume was the whole essence of spring in one tight bunch of cream and gold flowers.

There was also a small patch of violets. I had to search among the round green leaves to find the purple flowers underneath. I picked them for my mother, who had a beautiful evening frock just the colour of the violets. It was made of materials with lovely names — chiffon, and georgette — and it had a pattern of diamonds scattered on it like raindrops. My mother told me they were diamanté, made of glass, not real diamonds, but I didn't want to believe this. It would have spoilt the fairytale prince and princess story I wove about my parents in my mind.

The best thing about having a garden was that people gave me plants and cuttings. When the flowers appeared, I remembered the people.

I can remember going to a lavender farm to have Devonshire tea. I was disappointed with the spiky lavender bushes. The flowers were grey and dusty and their scent reminded me of linen cupboards.

But the strawberry patch was wonderful, with its starry flowers and glistening red fruits. The farmer gave us punnets made of pale thin ply-wood, and we were allowed to pick our own. We had to watch Bubba though. She decided she only wanted green strawberries in her punnet, and got in such a huff when she was told that she must only pick the ripe ones that she threw them away and stamped off to look at the fowlyard. My father went over to admire the hens too, because they were speckled black and white, and much more interesting than his white Leghorns.

The woman who brought us our scones and jam and cream on the verandah had a pink apron to match her pink face. When she heard about my garden she gave me two strawberry plants. They sent out runners, and next year there were four plants, just as the woman in the pink apron had predicted.

The best present I was ever given for my garden was the pussy-willow tree. One Sunday Bubba and I went for a drive with our parents. We stopped close to an old stone bridge which arched across a small river. I have forgotten the name of the river long ago, but not the face of the old man who came down his garden to his low dry-stone wall to speak to us. He had a knitted cap with a bobble on top, and a strange face that I didn't like to stare at too much. His mouth was so sunken in that his beaky nose and his chin almost met. His body was bent forward too, like an old tree that bends with the wind.

He talked to our parents while Bubba and I leant over the bridge. We were intoxicated by the moving water, throwing small twigs in one side, then running to watch them come out the other. I taught Bubba to call out: 'Pooh sticks!' If the old man hadn't read A.A. Milne he must have thought us very peculiar children indeed.

When we tired of this game, we went to stand beside our

parents, who were still listening to his stories about his early life on the farm. It was difficult to understand his gappy-toothed speech, so I became bored and leant over his fence to look at his garden. I could see some moss growing there, and it was the sharpest most brilliant green I had ever seen.

I asked if I could have a piece of it for my garden. The old man cut me out a square of it with the spade he was leaning on, and I was allowed to wrap it in my hanky. There was one snow-drop out in my garden at present. The little green dots around the edge of it made it seem too perfect to be real. I planned to plant the moss around the snowdrop.

'Mind you water it, girlie, it needs lots of water,' said the old man, smiling so widely with his gappy mouth that I was suddenly shy, and started fiddling with a small branch that was poking over the fence. It was part of a tall leafless tree whose branches criss-crossed towards the sky. Then I noticed the branch was covered with shiny pinky-red buds, and some of them were opening. They looked like the snouts of small, silver-furred animals emerging from their burrows.

I pulled back the sepals on one of them, so that I could stroke the soft grey fur, and the old man noticed. He noticed everything, although he blinked a lot.

He said: 'That's pussy-willow. Haven't you seen it before, girlie? Pretty isn't it? Like a row of kittens.'

I wanted to keep it, and he realised this and said: 'That will grow too, if you've got green fingers. Do you think you have?'

I looked at the hand that wasn't holding the moss. It was dirty — perhaps it even had a greenish tinge. I nodded, and he took a knife from his pocket and trimmed me off a piece.

'Now keep it in a jar of water until the little white roots appear, then plant it carefully. Give it room to grow.'

After we thanked him, we drove off waving, and he was still calling out: 'Mind you give it room to grow.'

I didn't of course. There wasn't space enough in my garden to take his advice. When it grew spidery roots inside the blue medicine bottle my father had found for me, I planted it between two strawberry clumps.

When I went back to Hobart years later and stopped to look at my childhood home, there was the pussy-willow, as tall as the two-storey house, and nearly pushing the back fence over.

And I could suddenly see the old man, leaning against his dry-stone wall, calling out to me: 'Give it room to grow.'

Bubba and Moira in the garden, 1929.

THE LAST TASMANIAN TIGER

Long ago, when I was a small girl in Hobart, my father and I had a regular outing on the Sunday mornings he was free from his medical practice. We went to the zoo.

It must, I think, have been a small and anomalous collection of animals, because in spite of these regular visits, there are very few of them that I can remember.

Certainly there were rabbits — hundreds of them, white, black, piebald, grey, brown and ginger, common or garden rabbits and exotic angoras. So prolific were they, and so soft-hearted their keeper in cutting back their number, that when I approached their wire-netting fence there was a *layer* of rabbits, perhaps three deep, all desperate to wrest a crust or piece of carrot from my hasty fingers.

There was also a pair of Bengal tigers, the pride of the zoo, whose cage, incongruously, was situated just opposite the poor rabbits, who must have shrivelled in fear each time one of the huge jungle cats emitted its great full-throated roar. The proximity of these two species was fortuitous, however, because my father was fascinated by the tigers, and spent his time murmuring 'Magnificent, absolutely magnificent,' and plotting how he could raise the money to have a fitting enclosure made for them, instead of the small heavily-barred cage which housed them.

If we disagreed about the relative merits of the family Leporidae and the large felines of the *Panthera tigris*, there was one animal about which we were in complete accord. We always ended up at the tiny — pitiably tiny — concrete yard with the rusted iron fence which contained the last of the Tasmanian Tigers in captivity.

'*Thy-la-cine* — a wolflike marsupial, *Thylacinus cyno-cephalus*', the label on his cage announced. 'Found in the forest areas of Tasmania, having dark transverse bands across its back, which suggested the name "Tiger" given it by English settlers. It is now verging on extinction.'

Scarred and moulting, his dull brown coat striped faintly with black like the shadows of his prison bars branded across him, he padded ceaselessly around his small enclosure. I can remember still how passionately I identified with this decrepit creature with the fierce, sad eyes; how I could sense, week by week, how his spirit was dying, his old heart breaking with the loneliness of being far from any of his kind who might still glide silently through the fern-fronded undergrowth of the Tasmanian wilderness, hunting in the shadows of the centuries-old Huon pines.

When I came across Ralph Hodgson's poem 'The Bells of Heaven', the 'tamed and shabby tigers' for which I would have knelt down with angry prayers were not the handsome prowling cats of India, but my small false tiger, with his sloping back and rickety hind legs. The pads of his paws were worn away by the concrete floor, instead of treading softly on the damp moss of the forests where age-old spirits still haunted the dark caves and deep ravines of the lonely mountains. When I knelt down so that his golden eyes were on a level with mine, they reflected such isolation, such knowledge of a deep and mystical past, that I felt I was in peril of learning some strange and terrible secret.

It was hard to explain to people how I felt about the tiger. My mother almost understood. She couldn't go back to the zoo after her first visit, she hated animals being in cages so much. She told the director of the zoo this in no uncertain terms when he took us to his house to see the baby lion cub he was rearing. She called the tiger a 'poor tosie', which must have been Gaelic and was what she called our dog.

When I told my governess Miss Crane about him, we started a new subject called 'Nature Study', and I wrote down things she told me in a blue exercise book. I found out something unique and wonderful about the Thylacine — it was a marsupial which meant the mother had a little pouch in which

44

she carried her cubs around when they were tiny. I cut out a picture of the Tasmanian coat of arms to paste in, because two tigers supported it. Good enough for the coat of arms, but not protected until 1936. Indeed, there was a bounty on their heads until 1909, because they took the farmers' sheep, and over two thousand were killed. How ironic that zoos today would pay a fortune for one of these animals, and naturalists and hunters carry on an obsessive but fruitless search to find one. The *Thylacine* roamed this earth over four thousand five hundred years ago, but modern man managed to extinguish him in a couple of generations.

There was some strange bond that held me to my tiger, because I even thought about him sometimes in the evenings after I was put to bed. The height of loneliness to me was going to bed in summer when it was still light. Outside my upstairs bedroom window, the sky was still a pale, pure blue, stencilled with the jagged green leaves of the big plane tree.

My parents came up to say good night, my mother sometimes in evening dress, violet or cerise, with pink roses at the low waistline, swooping to hug and kiss me, as exotic as some tropical butterfly or rainbow bird. She heard the four prayers I said every night, and my father read me chapters of *Winnie the Pooh*. I could read to myself of course, but it was much more fun when he did all the different voices and laughed so much.

After they had gone back downstairs, I got my lonely feeling. I sometimes used to creep out and sit on one of the stairs, just before they turned the corner, so I couldn't be seen, and I'd peer down through the banisters, listening to the various noises from below. My parents laughing and talking, maybe with visitors. Perhaps the gramophone was playing. Pots clattered in the kitchen if they were having dinner at home. If they went out, I sometimes crept down to the kitchen and Joyce, the maid, taught me fancy work, and I learnt lazy daisy and French knots, and helped her embroider the interminable doilies and pillow shams she was making for her glory box. But when she left, very suddenly, to marry her sailor boyfriend, crying for some reason I couldn't understand, I was more lonely than ever because Maud didn't encourage my night-time visits to the kitchen. She was engrossed with her *Peg's Paper*, an enthralling magazine about love, which I finally persuaded her to lend me, on condition I kept it under the mattress so my mother didn't know.

On the nights after Joyce left, and before I softened up Maud, I curled up in bed and roamed the wilderness with my Tasmanian Tiger, whom I had freed from his cage. We talked together about magical things, but I had always forgotten them in the mornings, as if they were only fading dreams.

Then suddenly, life became chaotic. We were going to move to the mainland. My father had bought a practice in Melbourne. I was excited, thrilled even, yet at other times sad and a little scared. Nanny cried, more over Bubba than over me, because she was still nearly a baby. She gave me a silver spoon with a map of Tasmania for a handle — the map of Tasmania was a very good shape for decorating things. Miss Crane gave me *Lamb's Tales From Shakespeare* and made me promise to send her some of the essays I wrote at school, because that was both a terror and a delight — I was to go to school for the first time. I was nine and had led an extraordinarily protected life, but now I was plunged into the heady delights of twenty-five new friends, a school uniform, lots more subjects to study, and extras like gymnasium!

No wonder that I completely forgot my secret friend, the poor old Tasmanian Tiger. It was with a real sense of shock, even of guilt, that I looked at an item in the morning newspaper that my father showed me one day in September, 1936.

DEATH OF THE LAST TASMANIAN TIGER IN CAPTIVITY it read, and the other paper stated LAST TASMANIAN WOLF DIES.

I hadn't given a thought to him for years — how could I have forgotten him for all this time?

Noticing how upset I looked, my father tried to cheer me up.

'Never mind, Moi, the poor old chap must have been a

great age, and probably in pain. And he's free of that rotten cage at last.'

And of course he was. That was the only way to think of him, my shabby old tiger, unconfined at last, his spirit free to join the ghosts of his ancestors from aeons past who haunted the lonely wilderness which is the true heart of Tasmania.

Moira (right) and her friend Juliet at Hobart Zoo, 1926.

*Moira in her Molly-O hat with some visitors at 'The Springs',
Mount Wellington, 1926.*

THAT'S THE END OF THAT

When I was about five years old, I had a black velvet hat. The crown was made in segments like an orange and it had a round stitched brim. I wore it inside the house as well as out of doors. It was called my Molly-O hat. I think it was sent to me from Ireland.

The greying photographs of me wearing my Molly-O hat were taken when my family were staying up at The Springs, on Mount Wellington in Tasmania. There were three elderly women in one of the photographs, and looking at this photograph brings the women back to me. How old they seemed, and they all wore black, but one — the fat one — had big pink roses all around her hat. She was the one, too, who wore white stockings, and her legs were fatter at the bottom than they were higher up. One was deaf and shouted things at me. The third one looked like an old eagle. She held on to her walking stick even when she was sitting in a chair, and when she laughed she thumped the carpet with her stick. I was frightened of her.

I was used to old people. My parents sometimes took me to visit elderly relatives, and I spent lovely summer Sundays trapped indoors. A Banksia rose tapped against a window, reminding me of the strange garden outside waiting to be explored. Birds flew against an oblong of blue sky. Sometimes there was the shrill alarm call of the blackbird to remind me there was probably a cat out there I could search for.

Even the strawberries and cream for afternoon tea, and the pastel-coloured sweets that tasted of talcum powder, didn't make up for those lost hours I spent indoors.

I wanted to be out finding my own strawberries among their starry flowers, or picking ripe raspberries carefully from the prickly canes. But I was conditioned to being polite to old people, and I realised already that they seemed to like to talk to children, that you could amuse them, and feel close to them.

I was used to old ladies, but these three old ladies at once, up at The Springs, were rather over-powering. They told me to sit with them and asked me about myself but they soon got onto my mother and father. Grown-ups always seemed to in the end.

The three old ladies took it in turns to ask me questions.

Why was I called Moira? Because it was Irish for Mary, and my mother was Irish. Ah, and was she a Catholic?

This was one of the questions I dreaded, because I didn't really understand what it meant. It was something my parents talked about when I wasn't meant to be listening. Ireland, and Catholicism and the Sinn Fein.

I drew a deep breath now and answered the three old ladies.

'She's not really Catholic just at the moment.' I added for good measure, 'She still belongs to the Sinn Fein though.'

This puzzled them enormously. It would have puzzled my mother too if she had heard me.

The three old ladies didn't tell me their names, so I named them in my mind. Deaf, and Fat and Walking Stick. I liked Fat the best because she told me how pretty I was, but I soon got tired of her hugging me. They had to keep repeating what I said to Deaf, who leant forward with her mouth open. It made some of the things I said sound a bit silly when they were shouted out.

Walking Stick had a dead animal around her neck. It had black fur sprinkled with silver, and it was holding its tail in its mouth.

Its eyes were glass eyes, teddy bear eyes. When it was alive I thought it would have had fierce dark eyes like Walking Stick. Its four paws, which had once carried it swiftly through the dark forest under the giant trees, hung down limp and hollow. I hated to look at it, so I looked down instead at Walking Stick's hands, both holding the handle of her cane. She had knobbly hands, with blotchy brown stains on the backs of them.

50

I grew tired of answering their questions. They thought they were being very clever, finding out all about my family and smiling at each other over my head. They didn't realise that I was cleverer than they thought, and some of the answers I gave were wrong on purpose.

I was becoming bored, so I asked if they would like me to recite to them. I had been given Edward Lear's *Book of Nonsense Rhymes*, and was starting to learn them by heart. I needed new tricks to keep attention focused on me, new ways to hold people's attention, because Bubba, my baby sister, was eighteen months old now. She had beautiful bright blue eyes and was rather solemn, so people did all sorts of things to make her smile. When she did, it was such a wonderful smile that they felt well rewarded, so it was better than if she had grinned and cooed all the time. She was sitting on my mother's knee across the room now, and someone was playing peek-a-boo with her.

I recited 'The Owl and the Pussycat' for the three women. When I finished, Fat hugged me, and asked if I knew any nice little prayers.

Walking Stick said suddenly: 'We are all in God's waiting room here.'

This gave me a strange feeling. It seemed just an ordinary room, very large, with a lot of people sitting about or standing at the windows looking at the view of the mountain. It didn't seem like God's waiting room, but perhaps she meant because the sky seemed so close.

I said I knew quite a lot of prayers, but I only said them in bed at night. I could see Fat was disappointed, but I really didn't feel like saying one.

I said I would sing them a song my father had taught me instead. I tried to think of one that would make them laugh.

I stuck out my stomach, pretending to be a fat man, and sang in as deep a voice as I could:

'Wot cheer', all the neighbours cried,
'Who're yer goin' to meet, Bill?
Have yer bought the street, Bill?'
Laugh, why, thought I could have died.
Knocked him in the Old Kent Road. Tra la la.

Walking Stick kept time by thumping her cane on the carpet, but it didn't make me like her any more. Fat gave me another squeeze, and Deaf said she would like me to sing it again, but louder, because she hadn't understood the words. I didn't blame her. I didn't understand them myself.

Then they started talking about my Molly-O hat.

'Why don't you take it off dear, so we can see those pretty gold curls that are peeping out,' said Fat. She tried to pull it off as she spoke, but I held onto it with both hands. I had just decided it was time to go back to my parents, when Walking Stick said suddenly: 'It's a funny hat for a little girl. Black. It's just like my hat, isn't it? Same shape, same colour.'

'Why, so it is,' said Fat.

I was shocked. Walking Stick was wearing an ugly hat pulled right down over her ears like a helmet. An awful hat.

'Well, that's the end of that,' I thought. It was an expression my father used with a sort of shrug and a smile when something was broken so badly that he couldn't mend it, like Bubba's Peter Rabbit mug when it fell from her high chair.

Well, that's the end of that.

I can't remember what I did with the Molly-O hat, but it disappeared. When it was time to go home, there was a great hue and cry because the hat was missing. People looked under the box pleats of couches, and took the cushions off armchairs so they could search down the back. All they found was lots of fluff and some hairpins. My father found a sixpence, and gave it to me. I think he felt I was upset about my Molly-O hat.

Going home down Mount Wellington in the car, I lay curled up on the back seat. My mother was nursing Bubba in the front, and mourning the loss of my hat, which she had loved.

'It's an absolute mystery' she said.

My father drove the car slowly down the winding mountain road. The engine made a chugging sound, and I fitted some words to its rhythm and sang them. I repeated them over and over again, under my breath:

'That's the end of that, well, that's the end of that.'

A PEA UP THE NOSE

I was reading Christa Wolf's book *A Model Childhood* this week, and her opening paragraphs struck such a chord in me that I thought about them for hours. She says that the past is not dead to us, but we deliberately cut ourselves off from it, as if we are strangers to the things that happened long ago.

How true it is that our brain plays strange tricks on us. I am often amazed by the way some past event, maybe way back in early childhood, has been buried in my subconscious mind for years. Then I happen to see or hear something that triggers off a chain of memories. They are usually small incidents that come seeping back, sad or funny, frightening or embarrassing, but all at the time they occurred must have caused me enough emotion to hide my head under the covers, both literally and metaphorically.

One of these past events occurred this week. Another small background piece of the jigsaw puzzle of my childhood slipped into place, when I was reading this same book of Christa Wolf's. I was enjoying the beautiful simple prose which she used to evoke her early years, when out of the page leapt a sentence about the child Nelly, who pushed a small wooden bead up her nose, in spite of frequent warnings not to do so. The sort of small incident which happens occasionally when children play with beads, and is only a drama if the bead cannot be dislodged by snorting and blowing.

And, back in time from over half a century ago, I remembered something about myself as a child of about four, maybe five, believing in fairies and given to reciting poetry whenever requested.

One late afternoon, I was sitting in one of my favourite places — halfway up the stair, before the staircase turned a bend. It was shadowy there, and had a lonely feeling. I can even remember that I was wearing a pale green viyella smocked frock and an angora cardigan. It was the colour of the pinky apricots in the garden. My mother had knitted it for me, and I loved it, especially the feeling of stroking the fuzzy wool up the wrong way, then smoothing it down again.

I could see the lighted hall at the bottom of the stairs, and beyond that the open doorway to the study where my parents and a few friends were trying out dance steps to the music of the new gramophone my father had obtained from Melbourne. It was probably playing 'The Desert Song' I imagine, because that was one of the few records they had at the time, and certainly the most popular. They played it over and over, and sometimes I couldn't get it out of my head, especially 'The Riffs' Song'.

It was an era a few years after the First World War when people had a sense of release. The end of being on active service in a foreign land in my parents' case. It was no wonder they had these occasional *thé-dansants* before dinner and learned the fox-trot, or played bridge or mahjong in the evenings to forget the past as much as they could.

There was nothing to stop me going down and sitting quietly on a chair, but I preferred to watch them from afar. I had been helping Joyce to shell peas in the kitchen, and I had been given a handful to eat raw. And then, when I had only one pea left, I pushed it up my nose. I wonder now whether I did it absentmindedly, or was it because I wanted my parents' attention? I was used to a lot of attention, and I have a feeling that maybe I resented being out on the sidelines. Whatever the reason, I was soon in a panic. My frantic blowing could not dislodge it, and if I tried to hoick it out with my little finger I only pushed it further up.

Finally I ran downstairs to my parents, crying and trying to explain what had happened. My father quickly realised what I had done, and told me he would be able to take it out in a moment, not to cry, it wouldn't even hurt. I couldn't stop crying though. My nose felt enormous, it felt as big as the whole of my face.

56

He reminded me of the poor Dong with the Luminous Nose as he removed the pea quickly with a little pair of forceps from his medical bag, but even that didn't cheer me up much although it was one of my favourite poems. The trouble was my nose was so swollen by then that I couldn't believe the pea had been removed until I was shown it sitting in a small kidney dish.

I was comforted with lemonade, which I was allowed to drink in one of the new cocktail glasses, crystal, with a long stem and so shallow that it was very hard to drink the lemonade without spilling it. I even had a cherry in it, on a toothpick.

But the whole episode must have made me feel ashamed as well as frightened. I can remember my father — usually so proud of me — saying to my mother afterwards: 'That was a strange thing for Moira to do. She's usually such an intelligent little girl.'

My mother replied that perhaps I was a bit bored and lonely. It would be much better for me when Bubba grew up enough to play with me.

I buried this incident for years and years — cut myself off from it — until I read Christa Wolf's story of the yellow bead. And then I felt that if such a famous woman of letters stuck things up her nose as a child — well, I needn't be too ashamed of it, need I? I mentioned I had remembered this small drama to my husband, and he said: 'But everybody did that sort of thing — what about beans in the ears? Don't you remember the popular song: "I think that my mother has beans in her ears"?'

Picnic at Brown's River, 1929. Bubba (left) and Moira (right).

PITY MICE AND PITY ME

The first family holiday I remember was at Brown's River. It was there I discovered sea anemones, rows and rows of them, red and green, lipping onto the narrow rocks with their fringed mouths sucking in the sea. I put my finger into one and felt it close up, trying to draw my finger inside it, turning into a glistening red blob, like a gummy toothless mouth. I found a mauve sea urchin, and long pink razor shells.

But the other thing I discovered at Brown's River was death. I knew the death of a white kitten, with a ribbon of blood coming from its mouth after the nursery fender fell on it. I knew the death of our sheep-dog Rover, when my mother sat on the laundry floor, holding his head in her lap and cried so much I wondered if she would care as much if I died.

This was going to be the death of a child. There was a boy lying in a bed on wheels on the upstairs balcony of the hotel. He had pale skin and blond hair and I went to talk to him every day. His name was Johnny. He had something wrong with his leg, and I never saw him out of bed.

'We can go and look at the anemones when you get better,' I said.

'I'm not going to get better,' he said. 'There is something wrong with the bone in my leg. I am going to die.'

I went to my father.

'Johnny says he's going to die,' I said. 'But it isn't true, is it?'

My father looked at me, weighing me up, assessing if I was old enough, strong enough, to take the truth.

'No, I'm afraid it's true, darling,' he said finally. 'Some time soon, maybe not just yet, Johnny is going to die. Poor little boy, he has a disease that we cannot cure yet.'

'But *you* can. You can make him better.'

'I only wish I could. There are some illnesses I cannot cure, some germs I cannot kill. Maybe one day, but not yet.'

Sometimes my father talked to me as if I was grown up. I was proud when he did, but scared at the same time.

Johnny showed me his leg one day. It was truly twice as skinny as the other one. I promised to write him a letter when we left, but he didn't answer.

When we returned home I developed a pain in my right leg too. Nanny said it was growing pains. For a long while I didn't tell my father, I was too scared he would say I was dying. But I stole the tape-measure out of my mother's work-basket, and measured the tops of both my legs in bed at night. Since I was determined to be a victim, my right leg was always thinner, because I held the tape-measure more tightly around it.

Finally, my father came in to say good night one evening, just as I was measuring my legs. It was an enormous relief to tell him I thought I was going to die soon. Just saying it aloud somehow made it seem less likely. I even thought he might laugh, but he didn't. He went down and got his surgical bag, and took out a little silver hammer. It had a rubber end on it. I sat on the edge of the bed, with my thin leg crossed over the other one, and every time my father gave my knee even a gentle tap, my leg jumped. I couldn't stop it doing this, and I started laughing about it. My father said it showed I didn't have Johnny's disease.

'Now how about your prayers?' he said. 'Mummy says she hasn't heard them tonight.' My mother had taught me four prayers, which I rattled off every night like a small, well-trained parrot.

There was 'Angel of God', and 'Jesus, Tender Shepherd hear me,' and the Lord's Prayer. I used to say 'Gentle Jesus', but I had gone off that one lately. Ever since my father asked in amazement:

'*What* was that you said, darling?'

Gentle Jesus, meek and mild,

Look upon a little child.
Pity mice and pity me,
And suffer me to come to thee.

I didn't like it as much when he explained about 'my simplicity'.

I said 'God Bless' many people that night, I was so relieved about my leg. I said: 'God bless Johnny.'

THE COMPANY MAKES
THE FEAST

One birthday my father told me he was going to bring home a new pet as a present. He wouldn't tell me what it was. It was to be a surprise. I thought it might be a kitten. We hadn't replaced the small white kitten which had been crushed by the nursery fender. Nobody seemed to have the heart to bring home another one yet, although the high iron fireguard with its shiny brass railing was now firmly hooked onto the wooden panels of the mantelpiece.

I was sure the pet wouldn't be a dog, because we had already talked about getting a puppy but my mother said we couldn't put old Rover's nose out of joint. It turned out to be two pets when my father unpacked a small crate he brought home at lunch time — a pair of bantams.

I loved chooks, and hadn't realised there were such perfect miniature specimens of them — a brilliantly coloured rooster, red-gold and brown, with an iridescent dark green tail, and a sober little hen with speckledy red-brown feathers. The cock was a little too arrogant to allow himself to become tame quickly. He wanted to strut and crow and parade around in front of the larger hens in the fowlyard. Luckily the little hen loved to be picked up, and have her neck stroked. She closed her eyes and make clucking noises under her breath in a soft, churring way. She seemed to have several sets of eyelids, and sometimes she rolled her eyes up in a strange way, but it was a sign of pleasure. She liked being wrapped in a doll's shawl and carried around, or wheeled in the doll's pram.

After a couple of months she laid her first egg in one of the nests used by the white Leghorns. It was a beautiful egg, brown, with a purplish bloom on it, and little bigger than a blackbird's turquoise egg I had found once in the grass. My father said she was still just a pullet, and her eggs would get bigger as time went by.

I wanted to keep it, but my mother said she had laid it especially for my tea. It was too small to fit in an egg-cup, but not really big enough to be a proper meal, so in the end I had to agree to have the top carefully cut off and the contents scraped out to add to the coddled egg I usually had for tea — soft-boiled, and mixed in a teacup with butter and bread-crumbs. Much nicer than the bread and milk we sometimes had instead. I hated it — the warm milk taste, and the sogginess of the bread. The only redeeming thing was the brown sugar sprinkled on it. I can still remember the relief when Bubba and I were considered old enough to change over to dinner at night with our parents.

My little hen wasn't popular in the house. Joyce refused to allow her in the kitchen, muttering about bird lice. I tried to remember to keep her outside, but there were times when I forgot. Once I brought her in while I was preparing a dolls' tea party. I sat her down on the kitchen table in her shawl, but while I was filling the tin teapot with water at the tap, she flew down and strutted around the floor. I was breaking up a biscuit when I heard Joyce's footsteps. She walked heavily, and talked to herself a bit, so you had plenty of warning when she was coming. I whipped Henny out the back door and into my pram.

When I went back to collect the tea tray, Joyce looked at me with suspicion.

'And what are you up to now?' she asked.

'Making a tea party for Daddy. He promised to have one in my cubby house,' I said, trying to look as virtuous and innocent as possible. Bubba and I had a wonderful cubby house under the pink oleander tree and the wistaria, which had so many twisted branches that you could sit on them like a couch. We often asked our father to come out and have tea when he arrived home, and each time I waited expectantly for the same joke. He dropped his cup on the dirt floor, and each time he said: 'Oh, I'm sorry, Mrs Jones, I seem to have spilt my tea on your second-best carpet.' I would have been very disappointed if he didn't make the same old joke each time, but eventually Bubba got quite upset about it.

Joyce said she would get me some milk from the ice-chest to put in my jug — it must have been one of her better days — and while I waited I happened to look down at the kitchen floor. There, on the polished dark green linoleum was a small black and white dollop. There was only one thing to be done. I walked over and stood on it, hoping it would stick to the crêpe sole of my sandal. Joyce didn't appear to notice anything unusual about my behaviour, but I picked up the tray to escape with my heart beating fast.

I don't know why I was so scared of Joyce that I sometimes got a strange sensation in the pit of my stomach. Certainly she never hurt me in any way, and wouldn't have smacked me, but perhaps there were times that she would have liked to. There was a feeling of resentment, stored up over the years, of life having been unfair to her, which expressed itself in the way she attacked the corners of the kitchen with her broom, or banged the pots and pans around.

'High falutin' ways, she's got,' she would mutter when my mother left the room, and crash would go another pan.

So I was glad to escape with my tea tray, but I had only just reached the verandah when she said:

'And what's this on my kitchen table, may I ask?' I had forgotten Henny's shawl, which Joyce pounced on and flicked off the table. And onto the floor smashed a small brown egg which she had laid while she was sitting on the table. Thereby ruining all the excuses I was thinking up about the shawl. Fortunately, Joyce, always unpredictable, thought this was funny and ended up snorting into her handkerchief and wiping her eyes.

It was a great relief because I never knew when she was going to get what she called 'scotty'. Or even worse. I knew that once she had been really angry with me, and had said 'Don't you dare tell'. I think she shook me a little. But tell about what? The memory of this only came back in little dribs and drabs. It was a bad memory, and it didn't want to come to the surface. It was to do with Joyce taking me to the beach one morning, when Bubba was a baby, and my mother stayed at home to mind her and look after the practice. Joyce's sailor boyfriend came too, and they made some sandcastles with me, then they left me to turn them out of my bucket by myself, and went further up the beach, and lay down in the sandhills.

We were very late for lunch. I can remember sitting on the bus stop and Joyce getting worried because we had missed the bus. My mother and father were upset because we were so late, and I was very flushed. They talked about 'a touch of the sun', and I was still sick next day. Joyce came in to my bedroom, and said to me again: 'Remember — don't you tell.' But tell what? I was scared that I would make Joyce angry by saying something she didn't want my parents to know, but I really didn't understand what it was, so I probably hardly opened my mouth for days.

Joyce was subdued after this outing. I think my parents had threatened to dismiss her, but she got a second chance. She was supposed to be getting married shortly to her fiancé, so I suppose they thought she wouldn't be there much longer. The trouble was, month after month went by, and her sailor didn't write to say he was ready to retire from the sea and buy a little farm, but finally one day my mother said to my father:

'Joyce got a letter today, and she's going to be married next month.'

My father said thank goodness for that, he had been beginning to think her fiancé wasn't going to settle down after all.

Perhaps I have been maligning Joyce, because when the time came for her to leave she wept noisily and hugged me so hard that I tried to wriggle free.

The new maid was called Alice and she became one of my best friends. She taught me to knit, and bought me a Knitting Nancy which was really a cotton reel with four nails hammered in the top. She gave me left-over pieces of pastry to make little treacle tarts, and even if the pastry got a bit grey while I was rolling it out, it tasted just as good.

She turned a blind eye to Henny coming into the kitchen in my pram, even when she became broody and hatched out two chickens as small as mice in one of the Leghorn nesting boxes. The chickens were allowed in the kitchen in the pram too, 'as long as I didn't make a welter of it', Alice said. It suddenly became *our* kitchen, and Bubba was allowed to have a good go at the pot cupboard under the sink.

It was funny the different feeling the kitchen had, with little cakes cooking in patty pans in the oven, smelling delicious, and the chickens making cheeping noises in the pram, half under their mother's wing. Even the blue kitchen clock with its black face and its tick that had seemed to get louder and louder and faster and faster, settled down and only made a pleasant background noise.

Alice wasn't as good a cook as Joyce at first. Sometimes her patty cakes were sticky on top, and sank in the middle. When she told my mother she was sorry about this, my mother just smiled. I could tell she liked Alice a lot more than she had liked Joyce.

'Never mind, Alice,' she said. 'Try using a bit more flour next time, and a bit less sugar. And remember — it's the company that makes the feast.'

I didn't know what she meant at the time, but years later I heard her repeat the old maxim while we were eating a particularly terrible wartime meal during rationing, and I thought back to that day in the kitchen in Hobart. The blue clock ticking away, the smell of freshly baked cakes, and the blue and white striped mixing bowl standing on the sink, with Bubba up on a chair, licking the last of the cake mixture off the wooden spoon. Alice and my mother were having a cup of tea, and I had my usual 'milk with a dash of tea'.

But what I mainly remember is the warm and friendly feeling in the kitchen on that particular day, and I knew exactly what my mother had meant when she said 'It's the company that makes the feast.'

AS HAPPY AS KINGS?

When Bubba and I were small, nothing sad or frightening was ever allowed to intrude in our lives if it could possibly be avoided. I can remember how shocked I was when, at the age of eleven, I was sorting through some old photographs and found a yellowed snapshot of a tiny grave. It was even possible to read some of the writing on it. It belonged to 'Denis Ralfe Giblin, the infant son of Margaret Norah and Arthur Giblin'. I had had an older brother, who died at Bright six days after he was born, and my parents had never told me this. Even when I asked, I could feel that it was something they found hard to talk about, this little baby who had died of forceps injuries after a difficult birth. It would have been better if he had always been mentioned over the years. As it was, I felt cheated in some way — things were not quite as they seemed, and this little dark shadow remained to haunt me. I had never grieved for him, and I wondered if perhaps, if I hadn't come across the photograph, I would ever have been told about him at all.

The stories we read were sometimes censored too. I still have a set of ten volumes bound in black with heavy gold embossing, called *Journeys Through Bookland.* My father bought them from a traveller when I was quite small, and my mother was a bit upset because they were printed in the United States, and were obviously edited for American children. Volumes 9 and 10, for example, are full of stories about American battles and things like the Impeachment of Warren Hastings. But I loved the first three volumes, which were full of nursery rhymes and fairytales. There was one poem in Volume I which my father had crossed out in pencil and initialled, so that nobody would read it to us. It was by Eugene Field, and it was called 'Seein' Things'.

It started off:

I ain't afeard uv snakes or toads, or bugs or worms or mice
An' things 'at girls are skeered uv I think are awful nice!
I'm pretty brave I guess; an' yet I hate to go to bed,
For when I'm tucked up warm an' snug an' when my
      prayers are said,
Mother tells me 'Happy dreams!' and takes away the light,
An' leaves me lyin' all alone an' seein' things at night!

And yes, certainly I know it all off by heart, because as soon as I could read to myself, it was the first page in *Journeys Through Bookland* to which I turned. I can remember the strange feeling in the pit of my stomach I used to get as I read about these things that come 'So softly an' so creeplylike they never make a sound!'

I felt this way because I did find it scary, and also because I was doing something my father had forbidden. It was so unusual for him to make any rules for us that the poem assumed a dark significance in my life it would not otherwise have done. So, in spite of my father's efforts to keep the harsher realities of life from me, the stuff of dreams and nightmares and figments of the imagination were more real to me than the everyday world.

There was comfort, though, every time I returned to *A Child's Garden of Verse.*

> *The world is so full of a number of things,*
> *I'm sure we should all be as happy as kings.*

I can remember saying that aloud, and feeling happy and secure. It didn't occur to me then, as it didn't seem to occur to the poet, that a number of those things were dangerous, sad, bad, even evil, and that kings, on the whole, were a sad lot. I stayed safely inside this cosy cocoon of security and ritual as long as I could.

Certainly:

> *It is very nice to think*
> *The world is full of meat and drink,*

70

> *With little children saying grace*
> *In every Christian kind of place.*

It's comforting, isn't it? So the shock is all the greater when the newspapers intrude at last, with pictures of children dead and dying of famine, and slaughtered in wars. But perhaps the children of our era were less damaged by the sudden onslaught of the outside world than the present-day young, who see so many news items of tragedy and despair, stick-like arms and legs and swollen stomachs, and tears shed until there are no more left to cry. So many news items that they have to switch off their emotions, while the horrors go mindlessly on. And therein lies the danger of the future — because if we all switch off our compassion, our true feelings, what hope is there for us all?

How much easier it was for me, sixty years ago, believing:

> *The child that is not clean and neat,*
> *With lots of toys and things to eat,*
> *He is a naughty child, I'm sure —*
> *Or else his dear papa is poor.*

The clothes that Bubba and I wore were also as English as possible. I can remember a little pair of gaiters, fawn, which buttoned up the sides of my legs. The only other place I can recall seeing gaiters was in illustrations in A.A. Milne's *When We Were Very Young*. In fact, when I objected to wearing my gaiters my mother explained to me that Christopher Robin wore them.

Our little tweed coats were English, as was the Molly-O hat. After that disappeared, my mother bought berets for Bubba and me. Blue for Bubba and green for me. I wanted the blue one, and persuaded Bubba to change, but my mother said this meant they clashed with our frocks.

Berets were coming into fashion then, but a lot of people didn't know how to wear them. My mother had an expert way of perching them on one side of our heads, and tweaking the front forward to form a brim, but when we put them on ourselves we pulled them down so that they looked like tea cosies on our heads. My mother had a constant war of the berets with Mary, the part-time nanny who sometimes took us for walks in the afternoons.

Mary pulled our berets down as hard as she could, trying to get them to cover our ears.

'You'll catch your death of cold if your ears aren't kept warm,' she said.

I was on my mother's side. My beret wasn't comfortable if it was pulled down, and I also rather fancied the idea of looking French. One day our father decided to take a photograph of us in our new berets, so Mary jammed them on our heads. I tried to explain to her that my mother would like us to wear them in the French fashion, but it was no use. She just kept muttering about 'Them Frogs'.

A BREATH OF THE
OLD COUNTRY

I was born and started to grow up on an island that was as small as an apple seed when I drew it in on a map at the bottom of Australia. But it was an island so large in my mind that the boundaries of it stretched away forever, past the great wilderness where the Thylacine roamed,

> *To the fairy land afar*
> *Where the little people are.*

I believed in fairies until I was in my teens. Writers I loved, like Robert Louis Stevenson and J.M. Barrie, seemed to take them for granted and I trusted in them. My only memory of going to see Peter Pan at the Theatre Royal in Hobart was being asked to save Tinkerbell by clapping if I believed in fairies. I found that I was still clapping after all the other children had stopped. I remember how embarrassed I was, and how my hands stung.

Apart from believing in fairies, there was another reason why the outside world seemed unreal in Hobart. I really had no feeling of identity with the Australian mainland. I grew up, as a writer friend once told me, 'as a little English transplant, in ignorance of exactly where you were'. It wasn't until we moved to Melbourne that Bubba and I became part of a more solid everyday existence. Until then I hadn't thought of myself as Australian at all. Small wonder, as we had governesses with English voices, and read books by English and American authors. I graduated from Christopher Robin, Brer Rabbit and *Alice in Wonderland* to Dickens. I had ploughed my way through the whole of Dickens by the time I started school in Melbourne at the age of nine, except for bits of *Martin*

Chuzzlewit which I found rather boring. It was a relief when I read aloud to Bubba from her Blinky Bill books, and all the May Gibbs books — back to the fairies again.

My mother said she would die if we developed Australian accents. There was no fear of that with all the elocution lessons we had. I knew how Eliza Doolittle felt about 'The rain in Spain'.

When my father and mother came to Australia at the end of the First World War, my father bought a medical practice at Bright, in Victoria. My mother told us later that she felt alien and depressed by the greys and browns and dull greens of the Australian countryside. She was even, she admitted, a little frightened of it. She was fond of reading D.H. Lawrence and would have agreed entirely with the letter he wrote his mother-in-law Frau Baronin von Richthofen in 1922:

> ...this is the land where the unborn souls, strange and unknown, that will be born in five hundred years, live. A grey, strange spirit, and the people that are here are not really here: only like ducks that float on the surface of a lake. But the country has a fourth dimension and the white people float like shadows on the surface.

But Tasmania was different from the mainland of Australia. Moving to the lush greens, the hawthorn hedges and dry-stone walls near Hobart was like coming home to my mother.

'Stop, stop a moment, Toby,' she would cry out as we passed apple orchards, pink and white with blossom, and small grey stone cottages, in later years when we were going for picnics.

'Ah, isn't it just like a breath of the Old Country?' she would sigh.

British people like my mother wanted to turn Tasmania into a small reproduction of that mother country so many thousands of miles away. Life on the small green island therefore had the feeling of a fairytale — of being one remove from reality.

The Scottish world of R.L. Stevenson seemed more real to me than the world around me. There I was, a Tasmanian child, reading poetry about mill wheels and organ grinders and Leerie the lamplighter. It was small wonder that when I started to write verses and stories at an early age, it wasn't of the natural things around me that I wrote, but of a white bird in England whose feathers fell as snow every Christmas, or a 'fairy on a mushroom brown', even a bunyip who flew from Tasmania to Loch Ness and became a monster.

I cannot remember a single Australian author whose books I read in Hobart. Until I went to school in Melbourne I had never heard of Banjo Paterson, Henry Lawson or Mrs Aeneas Gunn. There was no copy of *The Little Black Princess* in my bookshelf, but I knew 'Foreign Children' by R.L. Stevenson off by heart, and could have pointed out where these children came from on a map of the world.

> *Little Indian, Sioux or Crow,*
> *Little Frosty Eskimo*
> *Little Turk or Japanee,*
> *Oh! don't you wish that you were me?*

It didn't occur to me to wonder about the little long-lost Aborigine. I couldn't have done so, of course. The word 'Aborigine' wasn't even in my vocabulary.

THE PUFF BALL

'Can you see what I see?' asked our father, pulling his shiny Chevrolet to a halt on the edge of the road.

'Yes, yes, mushrooms!' shrieked Bubba and I. And indeed, the green paddock was polka-dotted with white caps. We had been holding our small wicker baskets since we left home an hour ago. Bubba had been clutching the handle of her blue basket so tightly that when she let it go now, to try to open the car door, her baby hand was criss-crossed with a pink and white pattern where the wicker had dented her flesh.

'Quick, quick, Daddy!' The door handle was too stiff for her.

'No, we can't just take them. We have to find the farmer first and ask him. Look, there's his house further along the road.'

The farmer was wearing a brown shirt and brown trousers to match his brown face. He was digging up potatoes in the vegetable patch next to his small white house.

Our father, a keen gardener himself, looked enviously at the piles of large potatoes, encrusted with dirt, and remarked: 'My word, you've got a good crop there.'

'Not bad, are they? Would yer like to buy some? Five bob a sack.'

My father produced his wallet, and explained that as well as the potatoes we would like to buy some mushrooms, which we would pick ourselves if the farmer was willing.

'Help yerselves. The wife and I don't fancy them. Nasty black mess they look when they're cooked. Yer don't need to pay.'

But his eyes rested wistfully on the pound note my father had produced, and he pocketed it quickly when told to keep the change.

'Take all yer want,' he shouted after us, and Bubba and I pranced towards the paddock chanting: 'Take all yer want, take all yer want.'

It was a golden day, which was unusual for that time of year when summer had ended and it was time for autumn's soft, lemony sunlight, as the days shortened into winter. There was a skylark singing high, high overhead, and in the grass were so many mushrooms that we could choose the very best. We picked the biggest, flattest ones with black frills underneath, until father explained to us that the small, rounded ones with delicate pink gills were the nicest to eat.

We were in a silly mood by now. 'Take all yer want', we called to each other, laughing each time we repeated it. Bubba wasn't looking where she was going, and she trod on a mushy cow-pat. She laughed so much she fell over, and lay in the grass helpless, spilling her mushrooms all over herself. I went to help her, but by this time she had turned over on her stomach and her lips were moving.

'What are you doing, Bubba?' I asked.

'Talking to a beetle. Look, he's black and shiny. His name's Alex... Alex'zanda. I want a matchbox to keep him in.'

'We haven't got a matchbox, Bubba. Besides, it would be cruel.'

'But Christopher Robin...' I was sorry I had told Bubba about Christopher Robin, it had made life more complicated.

Fortunately, at this moment father called to us.

'Come and have your photo taken, sitting on this nice smooth log with your baskets of mushrooms.'

Bubba got up. She loved having her photo taken and even allowed me to pull up her socks, and brush the grass from her smocked dress.

We sat together on the log, our arms around each other, our baskets at our feet. And there we are still, in the faded black and white print that I have, two little girls in smocked dresses, smiling at the camera.

'Come on,' said my father when he had taken the photograph. 'Time to go home. What a lot of mushrooms! Won't Mummy be pleased.'

Bubba was quickly gathering more mushrooms, over-filling her basket so that they fell out again.

'I'll just pick this one. Just this itty-bitty one,' she said. Unlike the other, it had a tough, leathery skin. Then suddenly it exploded in her fingers with a small 'pop' and a cloud of yellow powder came bursting out.

Bubba started back in alarm, and, as she usually did when she was upset, she started to put two fingers into her mouth.

'No, don't, Bubba,' said my father quickly, pushing her hand down so sharply that it was like a slap, and Bubba started to cry.

'Don't cry darling, it's all right. It's just that you picked a puff ball. It looks just like a mushroom, but it's poisonous. "Poisonous" means you musn't eat it, Bubba, so I had to stop you putting your fingers in your mouth.' As my father spoke he was carefully wiping Bubba's fingers with the clean, spare handkerchief he always carried in his top pocket. Because he was a doctor, he always stopped if we came across a road accident, and he had once torn his spare handkerchief into strips to stop a wound that was bleeding. It gave me a peculiar feeling in my stomach when I saw him taking the handkerchief out of his top pocket.

Bubba cried harder than ever, and I could feel tears sliding down my face too. My father noticed me wiping them away with the back of my hand, and said: 'It's all right, Moi. Bubba will feel better in a minute, she just got a fright. And she's not poisoned, she didn't put her fingers in her mouth, you know.'

But was *that* what was wrong? It wasn't really exactly what was wrong. My father knew everything, he had told me more than a million things about the world. He had told me about all the dangerous things. He had even called us over earlier that afternoon to show us an orange toadstool under a gum tree. It was shaped like the straw hats that Chinese people wore in pictures, and its stalk was thin and bendy like a strand of spaghetti. He had told us not to pick any of those, but — he hadn't explained to us about the puff ball.

When we got home I asked him to look it up for me in my encyclopaedia:

Puff ball: Any of various fungi of the genus *Lycoperdon,* having a ball-shaped fruiting body that, when broken open, releases the enclosed spores in puffs of dust. Some species grow to four feet across.

Why, that's bigger than I am, I thought before I went to sleep.

I had a dream that night, and was awakened by the echo of my own thin scream. My mother came running in, and called me 'alanna' and held me close. My father went downstairs and got me some warm milk.

Already the dream was receding, like the rim of a wave disappearing into the sands. The sea — the sea had been in my dream. The sparkling holiday sea at Brown's River. But it boiled and bubbled, and the red and green anemones which lipped the edges of the rocks had closed their waving fringes and turned black, and tiny, silver fish with diamond-bright scales lay gasping on the sand at my feet, with their red gills open. As quickly as I threw them back, they leapt out again, because it was boiling. The darkening purple black sea was boiling.

Then I saw it. The giant puff ball. It was enormous. It was bigger than the rising sun, it filled the whole sky as I waited for it to burst and scatter its evil, yellow dust.

'A nightmare,' said my mother, 'just a silly old nightmare.'

But how could it be just a nightmare when I could taste the acrid smell of it in my nostrils as I drank my milk?

I forgot about the giant puff ball for years. But on the sixth of August, 1943, as I stood in the kitchen listening to the radio spilling out the horrors of Hiroshima, I remembered.

Walking the floor, trying to warm my hands on my mug of coffee, I thought: 'Ah, so that's what it was about.'

DUCKS AND DRAKES

My childhood had a break across it as clean as a knife slash, and just as painful. It had a fascinated sort of fear to it too, the way the sight of blood might affect you. When I was nine we left Hobart, and moved to the mainland, leaving all our friends and even some of our toys.

I had lived for most of those nine years in a large brick house with an upstairs and a downstairs. Our waking and sleeping lives took place in different parts of the house, and I had a lonely feeling when I was put to bed at night. Years later, when I went back to look at the house in Sandy Bay, I was shocked at the way it had shrunk, as all childhood places one remembers tend to do. It was a tall, austere house of a particularly ugly shade of red, the front windows without eaves, so that it resembled a face without eyebrows.

The house we moved to in Brighton was a rambling Edwardian house with terracotta gargoyles on the roof ridges, and lots of stained-glass windows which cast faint jewel-coloured patterns on the pale grey carpet.

The bricks were almost smothered with Virginia creeper, so that its appearance changed with the seasons. The varying greens of spring and summer were replaced for a short while with the leaping flame red of autumn, and even in winter when the leaves had fallen, a tracery of black stems cobwebbed the bricks.

The house had eleven rooms, but two of them had to be used as a surgery and waiting room. The patients actually came to the house! Bubba and I were entranced. My mother wasn't so keen at first, but she gradually became drawn into the cosy ritual of popping into the waiting room to hear the latest local news. Some of the patients swapped recipes while they were waiting, and several were good with gardening hints, and

81

brought seedlings and cuttings for our garden. Others vied with each other to provide jars of marmalade with thin strips of orange suspended in the golden jelly. Or fruit cakes. My father was fond of fruit cake, and was lavish in his praise of such offerings, thus ensuring a constant supply of fruit cake in our larder.

The garden was the best thing about our new home. Very large and neglected, it had clumps of daffodils growing among the grass in the front garden when we arrived. There was a wonderful over-grown mirror plant, which made a perfect cubby house where we could spy on the patients as they walked up the front path. There was even a stable, with a loft and manger, a big shed for the horse and storing the pony trap, and the inevitable outside dunny with a long wooden seat.

Nothing gladdened my father's heart, however, as much as the sight of three fowlyards set along the back fence. Each had a grassy run, fenced with wire netting, and a henhouse with a galvanised iron roof.

'Chooks!' he cried happily, and we set off to see the man at the wood yard who also sold bran and pollard and wheat, and would obviously know where we could obtain some good laying pullets. Within a few days he supplied us with half a dozen white Leghorns — father's favourites — and half a dozen black Orpingtons, my mother having decreed that brown eggs, like brown bread, were better for us. The third hen run, to our great joy, was taken over by a broody hen who was given a clutch of eggs, and soon we had five yellow chickens. Bubba and I took turns to make their pollard and bran in the mornings. We loved the hot, steamy smell of it. Bubba even tried eating it, but said it didn't taste nearly as nice as it smelled, and she was sorry for the chickens having to eat muck like that. I thought to myself that she wouldn't have said a word like 'muck' when we had a governess, but I was secretly pleased, because I felt we were becoming emancipated.

My father also started working on the neglected vegetable garden, where over-ripe apricots and quinces rotted in the long grass, and shrivelled bunches of grapes hung on vines all along the fences.

He cunningly gave Bubba and me our own plots of land, and several packets of seed each. We slaved happily over our rows of carrots and silver beet, and waited impatiently for the mauve flowers to appear on our potato plants.

The strange thing about the vegetable garden was the number of bottles that were buried there. Green, rich royal blue, yellow and brown, each time we dug we found some more. Except for the odd one which was an unusual shape or a particularly rich colour, we threw them away.

The other mysterious thing about the vegetable garden was a large brick and cement hole in the ground, about eight feet square and three feet deep. Our father used to stand and look at this empty hole with exasperation. He dearly wanted to know why the previous owner had built it. Maybe to hold compost? If so, it had never been used for such a purpose, being clean and bare except for a few creamy blossoms from a nearby lucerne tree. Perhaps it was something to do with the horse, whose discarded horse-shoes were hanging in the stable, upside down, with all the good luck running out of them?

Finally, inspiration struck.

'Ducks!' said my father triumphantly, and put the hose in the hole to start filling it while he dashed up the street to consult the wood man again. We had eight fluffy ducklings swimming around the pond with their mother the next week, and all the small children who came to the surgery were taken out to see them as a treat after their injections.

Unfortunately, all too soon, the ducklings grew up into large Muscovy ducks, and became a mixed blessing. They laid a few eggs, but in secret places that were difficult to find. They failed to comprehend that the vegetable garden was their territory, and here they were meant to potter, providing rich manure and gobbling up the snails that attacked the lettuces.

But the fence dividing the vegetable garden and the back yard had collapsed under the weight of the Morning Glory that had swamped it in a purple-blue wave. The ducks, being gregarious creatures, marched firmly across it on flat, golden feet and took up residence on the verandah each day with the two cocker spaniels and the tabby cat. The rich manure which had been so desirable in the vegetable garden was much less welcome on the back verandah. Bubba and I were kept busy hosing it down because we were embarrassed when our friends came to play and got dirty shoes.

The ducks gradually disappeared, I don't remember how, because we certainly didn't eat them. They all had names, and we would just as soon have eaten the cocker spaniels or the cat. Finally only Jemima, the mother, was left, and in spite of our waning enthusiasm, father decided she was lonely and should have a mate. The wood man arrived with mallee roots for the fire, fresh supplies for the hens, and a drake tied up in a hessian bag.

It was making a hideous noise, and Jemima quickly waddled up to see what was going on. We all stood around as the man untied the bag and tipped the drake out onto the tray of his truck. We had scarcely time to give it an admiring glance, when, with a great flapping and whirring of wings it took off, and was soon only a mere speck in the blue summer sky. Jemima, thwarted of her mate, started flapping her wings too, and tried to follow him, but she was too fat.

The wood man was very upset about the whole thing, until my father told him that as the drake had been on our property when he flew away, my father would pay for him.

Jemima seemed to lose heart after this, and even went off her food. My mother had the brilliant idea of taking Jemima to the local park, which had a large lake in it. There was an island in the centre where wild brown ducks nested among the willow trees.

We took Jemima in the car, sitting on plenty of paper, and set her down beside the lake. She waggled her curly tail immediately, which showed she was pleased, then took to the water, swimming towards the island without a backward glance. The brown ducks were dabbling in the shallows over there, and she quacked eagerly as she approached them.

Bubba had second thoughts, and started calling loudly: 'Come back, Jemima duck, come back, come back.'

There was a gardener weeding nearby, and by now he was standing resting his foot on his fork, looking at us suspiciously.

We walked over to him, and my father explained that we had just donated a very nice duck to the park. The gardener was a bit taken aback, especially as Bubba was glaring at him and shaking her head. He looked around helplessly and waved at a notice on a post nearby. It was one of those depressing 'NO' notices:

NO dogs except on leashes
NO horse riding
NO bicycles

Fortunately there was nothing about ducks. My father gave the gardener ten shillings and asked him to please keep an eye on Jemima. This seemed to mollify him, and he agreed that the park was a wonderful place for ducks, what with all the water weed and the tadpoles and the children bringing stale bread.

We went back to see Jemima twice, but the third time we couldn't find her. We found the gardener though, and Bubba fixed him with her bright blue eyes and asked firmly what he had done with her duck. He looked a bit embarrassed, then said the truth was she had begun following him around the garden, and he had taken a fancy to her, so he took her home. We all looked at him suspiciously, but he went on to say that she got on very well with his cat, and liked sitting on his back verandah, so it certainly sounded as if he was telling the truth.

Bubba got a bit broody going home in the car, and kept talking about people who stole other people's ducks. She soon cheered up though, because when we arrived home we found our mother in the kitchen feeding two small kittens, one black and one pure white.

Someone had thrown them over our fence in a bag, probably knowing my mother was very keen on animals.

'Look, they're at least half-Persian,' she said.

We only had one cat at the time, so there was no trouble about keeping them. I let Bubba choose because she had been so good about Jemima, and she wanted the white one. We held our breath while our father inspected them for ringworm, but all was well.

In bed that night Bubba said suddenly: 'You don't think he *ate* Jemima, do you, Moi?'

'Certainly not' I said firmly. 'He gave us his address and said we could go and see her, you know.'

But somehow we never did.

KELMER THE HEALER

In that lazy-daisy haze of childhood there were at times clashing threads running through the pastel embroidery. Strands of gleaming scarlet invaded it when accident victims arrived dripping blood onto the waiting room floor. There was also a dark and more subtle thread, grey as a dusty cobweb, which partially dispersed after we moved into the house, but which lingered in shadowy corners late in the afternoons.

The place where this brooding feeling was strongest was in the outside laundry. I can still remember how my heart beat faster when I climbed the two wooden steps and stood inside, quite still, trying to absorb the eerie atmosphere, which seemed to dissipate as I concentrated on it. Sometimes there was the faint scrabble and squeaking of mice in the walls, but after that the silence settled thickly again. The trouble was I was ambivalent in my feelings. Sometimes, in spite of my curiosity, I wasn't brave enough to creep in without stamping loudly on the top step, or carrying the cat so that I would have an excuse for talking aloud to her. And each time, I was ashamed of myself for not being braver. There was a vast copper set in a brick fireplace and chimney, and the long wooden bench at the end of the troughs was stained with various dyes, the predominant one being a sulphuric yellow.

The copper itself gleamed darkly with the iridescent colours of an oil slick on water, its rim thickly tarnished with verdigris. There was a faint, strange smell that clung there, which I imagined might be the smell of sulphur. It reminded me of the way my hand smelled when I had been holding pennies for a long while in a damp palm. On the floor in one corner was a wooden box, filled with bottles of various colours. They were the same shapes and colours as the bottles in the garden.

I can remember the day when I willed myself to stay there,

my heart beating so hard that it seemed to be coming up in my throat, but my curiosity overcame my desire to run outside in the sunshine. I desperately wanted to pin down the feeling. Danger? Evil? Strong words, but I truly believed them. Suddenly my mother spoke behind me, and I jumped, pins and needles of fear running down to my fingers and toes as the adrenalin pumped through my body.

'There you are. I've been calling you for ages, darling. I don't think you should play in here.'

'Why?' So my mother knew too that there was something strange and haunted about the laundry. Fearful and yet relieved, I waited for her reply.

'Because the floor is dangerous. You could put your foot right through it. Daddy is going to have it repaired or perhaps pulled down.'

She spoke so matter-of-factly, but she gave me at the same time one of those shrewd, assessing looks that parents give their children when they wonder if they are being believed. My mother was Irish, and she knew better than I did that there was a strangeness about the room where we both stood in the gloom of late afternoon.

'Come along, I'm sure Linda would be pleased if you shelled the peas for her.'

A few weeks later I answered the front door during the school holidays. There was a tall old man standing there. He wore a dark, old-fashioned suit, and a striped shirt without a collar. He carried a shabby Gladstone bag, which clinked when he put it down as if it contained bottles. He said good morning politely, then asked if he could see Kelmer the Healer.

Kelmer the Healer! What a strange, mysterious name.

I told him that my father was a doctor, and that I had never heard of Kelmer the Healer. He was most upset, and explained that he had travelled all the way from Healesville with his horse and trap. He had last been to the Healer three years ago, and had now run out of all the remedies he had obtained. He had brought back the empty bottles to be re-filled. I asked him into the hall, and ran to get my mother.

Within a few minutes the horse was inside the back gate, having a drink and feeding on the long grass near the hen coops, and the old man was seated at the kitchen table, with a pot of tea in front of him, while my mother plied him with food and questions. As she cut up cold lamb, and shredded lettuce, decorating it with slices of hard-boiled egg and tomato, she asked me to get out the mint sauce, the bread and butter, and a clean napkin from the linen cupboard. He looked at the napkin very doubtfully, so I spread it across his lap for him, which didn't seem to make him feel any more at home.

'Tuck it under his chin, darling,' advised my mother, so I did, and he seemed relieved, and started on his food like a good child provided with its bib.

As my mother poured out cup after cup of strong tea for him, she started asking him about Kelmer the Healer.

Exactly how long ago had he seen him? What had Kelmer the Healer treated him for? What degrees did he have? What nationality was he? Was he old or young?

To every question, the old man, trying to be helpful, ended up seeming very vague and muddled. It was the same when my father came home for lunch and, enthusiastically, joined in the quest. At least he managed to ascertain that the old man was being treated for stomach trouble and rheumatic pains. The blue bottle was for the stomach, the brown one was for the aching limbs. The old man seemed sure about that. My father sniffed the empty bottles, seeking a clue to their contents in vain. And although he questioned the old man at length, and later went out and talked to his older patients, he never found out anything more about Kelmer the Healer. Nobody could remember whether he was old or middle-aged. Somebody thought he might have been an Indian. At least, he was brown-skinned. The one thing they agreed on, one day he was there, the next he wasn't. His elderly housekeeper, who hardly spoke when she answered the door, disappeared too.

The old man set off for Healesville with his trap laden with ripe quinces, apples for the horse, a piece of homemade orange cake to eat on the way, and several free samples of stomach powders and arthritis pills. We never heard from him again.

The night after we learned about Kelmer the Healer, Bubba thought she heard someone in the garden outside her window, and became scared because she thought he had returned to bury some more of his bottles. Bubba was very good at thinking up excuses for getting into my bed and being told a story.

The weeks went by. Linda's fiancé wrote to say the wheat crop was a failure so his father couldn't pay him a wage for a while, and they might have to postpone getting married. Linda went into her room to have a good cry, but cheered up when my mother gave her a week off to go and see her fiancé, and paid the return fare for her. When she came back she bought a lot more transfers of lovers' knots and started to embroider her nighties.

We gradually forgot about Kelmer the Healer. We had a gardener one day a week by then, because my father's practice was busier, and Bubba and I had lost our first enthusiasm.

One Saturday morning when I went out to tell Harry that his morning tea was ready in the kitchen, I found him with one foot on his spade, shaking his head as he looked down at a small dirt-encrusted pile beside the trench he was digging. Dark green, and brown, and deep, deep blue the bottles shone where the sunlight penetrated through to the glass.

'I dunno,' he said. 'However many times I dig over this garden, I always find a whole heap more of these here bottles. I'm darned if I know where they come from.'

THE BIG OLD EAGLE

When we first came to Melbourne, Bubba and I stayed with Gran and Aunt Marjorie for a few weeks while our parents drove around Victoria looking for a practice to buy.

Gran decided that we would go to St Paul's Cathedral as a treat. She probably felt too that our religious education had been neglected. It was exciting for two reasons, that Sunday outing. We had never been in a train before, and also never visited a cathedral, which I imagined to be very like a large castle, only better because it belonged to God.

The train went very fast between the stations, its *rackety-rack* growing louder and louder as it went faster and faster. I thought back to Robert Louis Stevenson and repeated to myself:

> *Faster than fairies, faster than witches,*
> *Bridges and houses, hedges and ditches;*

I had always thought it a sad poem, because the last line was: 'Each a glimpse and gone forever!'

Sometimes the train ran along a high bank, and we looked down on back yards where children played and dogs chased balls and fathers dug in their vegetable gardens. Some of the yards had small outhouses with lavatories inside them. There was even one with the door open, and a little girl sitting inside it, which seemed rather rude.

I turned to look at Gran to see if she had noticed, but she was humming quietly to herself, with a faraway look in her eyes.

Some of the people we went past in the train didn't even look up to watch us travelling past to the city. Bubba was sitting at the other window opposite me. She waved to one little boy who stopped playing to watch us, but he didn't wave back. The stations were almost as interesting as the back yards, with huge billboards on the walls. They didn't give you time to read them all though. Swallows' icecream 'at the sign of the flying Swallow', Hutton's hams with a man pushing another man in the face, saying: 'Don't argue, Huttons *are* the best', Dad Washing Tablets, Reckitts' Blue, and a brown man advertising Bushells' tea. On and on they went, with beautiful ladies and men in yachting caps smoking cigarettes, Capstan, de Reszke, and Craven A with a black cat on the packet.

Before we arrived at the city Gran gave Bubba a little talk about keeping quiet and sitting still in church, and putting her sixpence in the plate when it was passed around. (I thought for a moment she wasn't going to part with her sixpence when the time came. I could see it was a struggle, and I was very proud of her when she dropped it into the silver plate.)

The cathedral was just opposite the station, which was why Gran had decided to come by train. I had never seen so many people, and I couldn't imagine Gran walking far in such a crowd. Gran always walked rather slowly, and held a walking stick with a beautiful ivory handle, although I don't think there was anything wrong with her legs.

As we left the station there were rows and rows of clocks, all telling different times. There were people standing around under these clocks, which was really puzzling because they all looked so bored. I asked Gran what they were doing, and she said: 'I believe a lot of people arrange to meet their friends under the clocks, dear,' as if it was rather a strange thing to do.

Gran needn't have worried about Bubba behaving in church. Peering around Gran's erect navy blue figure in the pew, I could see Bubba, hemmed in by Aunt Marjorie on the other side in case she decided to go wandering up the aisle. She was completely absorbed as she gazed at the ceiling arching high above us, and the rich stained-glass windows. Jesus, surrounded by little children and lambs and flowers, looked far better than he did in the pictures in my Arthur Mee's *Children's Bible*. Bubba's fair hair curved forward around her cheeks under her fuzzy wuzzy beret. Her cheeks were bright pink with excitement, and her eyes were wide with amazement.

Everybody stood up and sang a hymn, but I just moved my mouth and pretended, because I didn't know the tune. Then the minister, who had been standing in front of the altar, moved across to the side of the cathedral, and climbed up to his lectern to read the lesson. As he turned the pages of his Bible, which was spread out on a beautiful brass eagle, Bubba started to fidget. Then she turned to Gran, and said in a clear and carrying voice:

'Gran, I do wish that big old eagle would get out of the way, because I can't see God properly.'

Moira, a neighbour, Bubba, Aunt Marjorie and Gran (standing) outside the potting shed. Melbourne, 1931.

NEVER A MOMENT'S PEACE

'There's never a moment's peace,' my mother used to complain sometimes. It was a cry from the heart, and unfortunately all too true. Both my parents were bound to the medical practice by invisible chains, and to a certain extent Bubba and I were too.

'Who's going to mind the house?' was the constant cry as we grew up. By minding the house we meant minding the practice of course, and if you had volunteered to be the one to stay home, you couldn't even go out in the garden because of that demanding telephone.

The patients influenced our lives, the surgeries held at the house twice daily seeped perpetually into our consciousness. Physically, we lived with the smell of antiseptic and methylated spirits and ether. I could always tell when I kissed my father if he had been giving anaesthetics that morning — his cheek felt cold and slightly damp, and the faint sickly odour of ether clung around him.

We were a demonstrative family. I could tell that my school friends found it strange when they came to play that we called each other 'darling' and kissed each other if we had been separated for a few hours. We all worried about my father because he worked so hard, and we waited on him hand and foot. Early in the morning we all combined to get him off to his anaesthetics and tonsillectomies. He was inclined, my mother said, to potter. On the contrary, replied my father, being relaxed was the secret of a long life. While he stayed relaxed we all panicked and the clock ticked away.

We shut up the cocker spaniels, made sure Jemima the duck was temporarily penned up to keep her safe from the car wheels, and opened the back gate. A final flurry to find the car keys — 'I know I had both sets a moment ago' — then we sank back exhausted for a few moments after he left. By then Bubba and I would realise we were going to be late for school if we didn't hurry. The telephone would always start ringing at this stage.

'You go, Moi,' my mother would urge if Linda wasn't nearby to answer it. 'It will be the hospital to see if he is on his way. Tell them he left ten minutes ago, darling. I can't face them again.'

By lunch time, after a round of visits when the operating was over, our father would return home flagging a little.

Linda or my mother provided him with a nourishing lunch, always a difficult meal.

'Just a bit of bread and cheese will do,' he would say, but he would have been very surprised to sit down to anything less than home-made soup in winter, followed by an omelette, or something in white sauce, perhaps whitebait or chicken leftovers.

He would have been surprised too if he hadn't sat down to a well-set dining room table, with fresh flowers and his starched napkin in a silver ring. The tea tray would be on the sideboard, the silver teapot ensconced in a knitted tea-cosy with a china lady sitting on the top (an offering from an elderly patient), the milk jug with its netting cover edged in crochet decorated with bright blue beads (another present from a patient).

By the end of the afternoon surgery he was flagging again, until he developed a clever trick of slipping out between patients to have the pick-me-up we made for him. Whoever was home shook up in an aluminium shaker a mixture of milk, Milo, yeast, and a vitamin supplement which tasted of cod-liver oil and chocolate. My father swore by this concoction, saying it bucked him up immediately, and maybe he was right because he practised until the age of seventy-nine.

He pottered in his garden for a while before fitting in another house call or two before dinner. It was the evening surgery that was what my mother called 'the killer'. It was hard for us to relax and do our homework, or sit and read when there were people roaming around the front of the house. The patients didn't have appointments, they came and let themselves in the front door, and sat in the waiting room awaiting their turn, so it was apt to be a feast or a famine. Sometimes they overflowed into the sitting room, or cunning ones stationed themselves on the chair in the front hall, so that they could crash the queue. Tempers flared if this happened, and my father had to try to be very diplomatic.

It was a relief when the door shut on the last patient. My father often put his head down on the surgery desk, and had 'forty winks' at this stage, and my mother, who was waiting to go in and do the accounts, was torn between letting him have a sleep, and getting on with the bills, which were a necessary evil, and which she hated.

That was, hopefully, the end of the day, but sometimes the thing we dreaded happened. The telephone would wake us all in the small hours of the night. We understood the necessity if it was one of his mids going into hospital, but my mother dreaded the occasions when he went off to cope with a situation that involved domestic violence. Doctors seemed to fill so many roles in those days. I nearly always stayed awake until he came home again, listening to my mother roaming around. Sometimes I slipped out to the kitchen where she would be having a cup of tea, the cocker spaniels waiting with her to prick up their ears on hearing his car. Sometimes he would be grey with fatigue when he came in.

'Toby, it's not good enough. It's too much,' my mother would say, and my father would inevitably laugh and reply: 'Ah well, there's no rest for the wicked.'

THE FACTS OF LIFE

The small friendly school Bubba and I went to when we settled in Brighton was, unfortunately, only a primary school in those days, so when I was twelve I had to change my grey tunic for a navy blue one, and face another sea of new girls.

The new school was also fairly small and relaxed, but it was hard to break into a group of girls who had already spent six or seven years together. However, I had realised by now that you were considered a 'goody-goody' if you seemed too enthusiastic about your lessons, and always did exactly as the teachers told you to. I tried very hard not to conform too much, and I even tried not to come top in exams.

Gradually I managed to become friendly with the group of six girls I had admired from my first day there, and I was immensely excited when one of them slipped a pink party invitation into my hand. They had at last accepted me. It didn't even seem to matter that I had to wear such a childish party dress — white voile, sprigged with flowers, and a sash, and that I still wore white socks and black patent shoes with straps. My heroines wore frocks that were miniature copies of their mothers' clothes, and silk stockings, held up by suspender belts which one of them was kind enough to show me. I think they adopted me as a sort of mascot. I was small for my age at twelve, although I shot up later, and I was eventually the only girl in the class who didn't wear a bra. I looked up my father's medical books to see if there were women who never developed what I thought of as 'bosoms'. 'Breasts' seemed a terribly indelicate word in those days.

Although they called me 'little Gibby' and were slightly patronising towards me at first, I soon realised this group of friends wasn't nearly as sophisticated as I had supposed. They just put up a good front, and sometimes covered up their ignorance by bluffing. Lying under the peppercorn tree at lunchtime we had long discussions about life and what it would be like to be in love. Sex inevitably cropped up, and was a constant worry to us, because there was no sex education in schools, no Mother and Daughter nights, no television programmes with films to enlighten us, no explicit magazines that we could buy.

One day there was a heated discussion about whether babies came out of your navel. The girl who was trying to convince us of this said of course they must, or what was the point of *having* a navel?

Now, I wasn't exactly certain about how the father put the seed into the mother, but I certainly knew how babies were born. You couldn't live in a general practitioner's household with a father who delivered babies and not know something like that. Sometimes, if my mother or the maid were outside, I even had to answer the telephone, and if the caller was a nurse from one of the local hospitals, I had to be very careful to take down all the details of my father's midwifery cases. I would ask how far apart the pains were. For some reason I felt very embarrassed if the nurse mentioned that the waters had broken. Then we would have to track down my father from the list of patients he had left when he went out on visits. I used to get really upset until we had managed to contact him.

Although I had acquired a lot of information, it was a bit muddled, and I realised it would be better for my friends to be given expert advice. It was time to borrow one of the books about obstetrics and gynaecology from the glass-fronted bookcase in the surgery. This turned out to be quite an enterprise. Some of the books were too large to fit in my schoolbag unless I left my homework and my lunch at home. Most of them weighed a ton, and some didn't have any diagrams or photographs.

I finally found one that seemed fairly suitable, and moved the rest of the books along so that there wasn't an obvious gap. Looking back, how stupid the whole exercise was. My father was a very liberated man, and if I had mentioned it I am sure he would have suggested to our headmistress that he would give us a talk about reproduction.

He asked me sometimes if there was anything worrying me, or if there was anything I needed to know, but I always said no.

Anyway, my friends were much impressed by the medical book, which squashed the navel theory once and for all. My stocks were high after this and I felt most sophisticated and grown up.

But pride certainly comes before a fall.

One day I received a letter in the post from Jill, the editor of the daily children's page in *The Herald*. She said that she had been lent a large exercise book of stories and poems. A friend of my father's had shown them to her, and they planned to put them in 'The Herald Junior' as a surprise for me. She ended her letter:

'I think there must be two Moira Giblins — one who often could be found wandering quietly in places where the bell-birds nest.'

Help! It was a very kind idea, and my parents seemed pleased about it, so I couldn't possibly hurt the feelings of all the adults concerned by asking if Jill could please stop publishing my writing every day or so. To make matters worse, some of these stories and poems had been written several years earlier, and were positively full of elves and fairies.

Even the five shilling postal note she enclosed for the first story, which they were printing that evening, although it was a princely sum in those days, didn't compensate for the amusement and scorn I imagined my peer group would feel.

I used to dread going across to the shop to buy my father his *Herald* each evening, and yet it was exciting too to see my name in print. Most of the pieces were illustrated, which made them look quite professional. The supply of postal notes too, provided me with all sorts of things from books to budgerigars, that my shilling a week pocket money wouldn't run to.

The girls at school were kinder about it than I had imagined they might be, although one of them did ask with a snigger:

101

'Seen any fairies lately, Gibby?'

I was ready for this. 'Oh, you saw that old thing, did you? I wrote it years ago. Oh, by the way, in my father's surgery there's a very interesting book about contraception by Marie Stopes, and I thought I might bring it to school tomorrow.'

And that settled things very effectively, even if Marie Stopes did turn out to be a bit of a disappointment. All those chapters about douches and sponges and vinegar and so on — I can remember we looked at each other in dismay, and Bonnie said: 'Surely there must be more to love than this.'

It was the last book I borrowed from the surgery. I felt responsible for the depressing effect it had on us all. I didn't want to put them off the whole thing. I can even remember thinking: 'It was better when I believed in fairies.'

BANANAS

Bananas must have been an expensive luxury during my early childhood. My grandmother used to repeat a small incident which she found very amusing, but I didn't find funny at all. When she had come to stay with us in Hobart, she had taken me for a walk and bought me one banana. She carried this home in a paper bag, while I danced around her saying: 'I want it now, please Gran.'

To which she quite properly replied: 'No dear, when we get home. Nice little girls don't eat in the street.'

'But I want it now...' and so on, all the way home.

I got my chance to feast on bananas when we were travelling across Bass Strait in the *Niarana* to make our home on the mainland. It was a rough trip. Too rough to go in to dinner, so we sat in the cabin and I ate large quantities of bananas.

It was a terrible night, because somebody in uniform knocked on our door and said there was a radio message for my father. The message had been sent to Hobart, but it had missed him. It was from the doctor from whom my father was supposed to be buying a practice in Perth, saying he had changed his mind about selling. And here we were, on the way!

It must have been hard to find a medical practice to buy in those days, because I can remember my parents being very upset. I was nine by then, old enough to realise the upheaval this move was causing to our lives, and the fact that we no longer had somewhere to go gave me a strange, lost feeling. It changed the whole course of our lives, because we finally ended up in Melbourne instead of Perth.

The other thing that happened that night was that I ate far too many bananas and was violently ill for the rest of the night.

My illness took my parents' minds off the radio message for a while at least.

You would think that might have put me off bananas for life, but it didn't seem to at all.

I can remember my mother handing me a shilling one day after we had settled in Brighton, and asking me to go across the street to buy a lettuce. We had eaten all the ones my father had planted, but we still had plenty of tomatoes. In those days you didn't tear up lettuce, you shredded it very finely with a sharp knife, and it lay on the plate in wavy lines with about three slices of tomato on top, and a slice or two of hard-boiled egg.

When I came back with this particular lettuce, which had cost threepence, I had spent the change on a bag of bananas.

'The greengrocer said they were particularly good today,' I told my mother, who was stirring mayonnaise in a double boiler on the stove.

'Hmmmp, he's feeling the pinch too, is he?' she replied, and I could see she wasn't very pleased. I felt guilty about the bananas, because I hadn't needed much persuading. I still had a fondness for bananas which was almost a craving.

'Did you mind me buying them?' I asked.

'Well,' she said, 'it's all right, but I really needed the change for your school lunches. Also, there are a lot of apricots to be eaten up at present.'

I can remember feeling quite shocked that we were so short of money. Bubba and I took fruit and home-made cake to school but we were allowed to buy a round of sandwiches each at the school tuck shop, because our bread was a bit stale and crumbly by the mornings.

We were supposed to have brown bread, and we generally ordered vegemite and walnut sandwiches, which we loved, but every now and then we succumbed to the white bread and Stras sausage with tomato sauce which many of the girls favoured. Being forbidden because it wasn't so good for you, it seemed specially delicious.

People expect doctors to be wealthy, or at least reasonably well off, but we certainly weren't in the early years after we moved to the mainland. The country was in the middle of a depression — a mysterious thing which I struggled to understand. My father was striving to pay off a house, build up the small practice, and to help support his mother and sister.

We had a funny second-hand car called a Willys Knight tourer. It had side-curtains which buttoned on and were made from mica which was so scratched that they were difficult to see through. When Bubba and I needed bicycles to ride to school, we went to the bicycle shop with our father and bought second-hand ones, and the owner was quite indignant.

'I thought a doctor would be able to afford new bicycles,' he said, and I can remember feeling embarrassed.

Every sixpence counted. The private patients paid ten shillings and sixpence for a consultation, the Lodge patients paid only a guinea a year for all their treatment. My mother used to complain that when some of the patients came to pay their bills, they put a ten shilling note or a pound note in the envelope with the account, and didn't bother about the extra sixpence or shilling.

There was one wealthy patient in particular who did this, and she always came to the house in person to pay her account, hoping, my father said, that he would happen to open the door to her, and she could get a bit of a free consultation while he was writing her a receipt. I felt very indignant about this, because I could see how hard my father worked, and one day I happened to open the door to this particular patient. I was about twelve by then, and had been taught how to give a receipt.

There was a ten shilling note in the envelope with the account. I decided to be brave, and drawing a deep breath I told her that the money was sixpence short.

She took the envelope back from me, and horror — there was a sixpence that I had missed tucked down in the corner of it.

She gave me a terrible false smile, and said in a sweet voice that she wondered if I was a little young to be giving receipts. It was the sort of thing that was so embarrassing that you put your head under the pillow if you thought about it in bed.

We were lucky that we had so much land that we could have

a big vegetable garden, and there were five fowl pens so we had our own chooks for eggs. We never killed our own fowls to eat, but we bought one very reasonably every week from one of the patients. Chickens were so much better then. That was something my sister remembered about our childhood when we were talking about it recently. The plump chickens which had so much more flavour, and there was plenty on them for a meal even when our grandmother and Aunt Marjorie came to Sunday dinner. These days they seem to taste of string, and to have melted away in a puddle of water in the baking dish.

During the summer we had stewed fruit from the garden nearly every day. The apricots and plums were all right, but I could have done without the quinces, even if the tree had the most beautiful blossom of all in spring — large delicate pink and white flowers, outshining even the apple blossom in their starry beauty. I am sure my mother could have done without the quince tree too, because her conscience made her boil up some of the unripe quinces for jelly. It was such a performance, wiping the brown fuzz off the unripe fruit, and hanging it when cooked in calico bags in the pantry to drain until next day, then adding sugar to the juice and boiling it again and waiting apprehensively to see if it jelled.

'It's *almost* worth it,' I heard her say once, holding a jar of red-gold jelly up to the light.

The ripe quinces, stewed, were a beautiful colour too, but I hated the way they made my mouth feel furry. I asked if I could make a junket to have with them, and by then we were having a fourpenny bottle of cream each day, which disguised them a bit. If you swirled the red-gold juice around in your sweet bowl with the cream, it made beautiful patterns.

I was fascinated by junket in those days, crushing the little rennet tablet with the bowl of a spoon, and being careful it didn't shoot across the room. It was crucial to have the milk at blood heat, not too hot or you had wasted a pint of milk. I used to cheat a bit, by sticking my finger in to tell if the milk had reached blood heat, but I always washed it first. When the Miss

106

Muffet-flavoured varieties of junket came out, it was much easier, and fascinating as the milk turned the crystals to pink for strawberry, yellow for lemon, or white for vanilla. Once I started biology at school though, and learned that the rennet in junket came from the stomach of a cow, I couldn't eat it again.

During our early years in Melbourne, Bubba and I had very few out-of-school clothes. A velvet frock with a lace collar for winter for best, and a sprigged voile for summer. They had marks around the hem where they had been let down. We didn't go to the department stores to buy clothes; my mother found a patient who did some dress-making at home. I hated being fitted for a new dress, although the dress itself, when finished, was a big event.

The dressmaker had a cold sitting-room where she fitted us, and her fingers were icy, although she only touched us with the tips, pinning in the sleeves, fiddling with the neckline. She kept the pins in her mouth, and I thought she would swallow them. She had funny breath that smelt coppery like pennies, and she took ages to pin and re-pin the hem.

'I'll make yours a bit long, dear,' she would say to my sister. 'You're growing at such a rate,' so poor Bubba had to pay the penalty of having to 'grow into' her new frock for the sake of not letting down the hem too often. I tried to console her by telling her that if she didn't have such long legs she wouldn't win all the races at school. She took after our father, and was very good at all sports.

The dressmaker's children weren't allowed in the room when we were having a fitting, but every now and again, their heads bobbed up behind a dusty pittosporum bush outside the window when her back was turned. There were boys as well as girls, and I was terribly embarrassed if I was in my petticoat.

The greengrocer who sold me the bananas also had a glass showcase full of sweets. Licorice blocks, musk sticks and little packets of sherbet which you sucked up through a licorice straw. There were even pink and white false teeth, which fascinated Bubba. I tried to resist all these, because he had a newsagency too, and I needed to buy threepenny exercise books quite often with my pocket money. In them I wrote stories and poems, and on the plain white pages I drew pictures of fairies, trying to imitate the drawings of Ida Rentoul Outhwaite. The fairies generally sat on mushrooms, their wings neatly folded behind them. It was too difficult to draw them flying.

After much cajoling, we were allowed to order a comic each. At first Bubba got *Chick's Own* every week, and I bought *Tiger Tim's Weekly*, but I soon grew tired of the Bruin Boys at school and changed over to *Schoolgirl's Own*. The lucky schoolgirls often seemed to go to school at haunted Granges, or have mysterious Indian princesses as boarders. They even had crown jewels hidden away in their lockers, and faithful servants who appeared from nowhere to do their bidding.

Fortunately my mother paid for the *Australian Women's Weekly*, or I might have had to sacrifice my comic to buy it, because it had a full page of Mandrake the Magician. I was in love with Mandrake, who had shiny black hair with one lock falling carelessly over his forehead. He had the thinnest of moustaches, and narrowed eyes which gave him a slightly sinister expression. The artist drew clever slash lines down his cheeks, which gave him interesting high cheekbones. He had a girl friend called Princess Nada or Nardine — something like that. I know it reminded me of sardines. He also had a manservant called Lothar.

Our maid Linda liked him too, and I took the *Women's Weekly* out to her as soon as I'd bought it each week. In real life Mandrake would have had that black, well-oiled hair that looked a bit like patent leather, and glittering dark eyes like Ramon Navarro, who was one of our favourite film stars in Linda's film magazines. When I said this to Linda, she said 'Ooooh, I'd love to meet someone like that,' and I realised that her fiancé Neil would have very little hope if someone like Mandrake came along.

As well as the *Women's Weekly* we bought *The New Idea*, and Linda read all the funny pieces people wrote in about their lives, and cut out the helpful hints about removing stains and what to do with left-over vegetables. She stuck them in a pink and gold-covered book I had given her for her birthday. She wasn't allowed to cut out the hints and recipes until the magazines had been in the waiting room a couple of weeks, and sometimes, to her annoyance, the patients got to them first, and tore out whole pages.

One day she said: 'Look, here's something to do with over-ripe bananas', and read out an article called 'Helpful hint for Hoyas'. You mashed up the banana and spread it around the hoya as a fertilizer.

Then she started to giggle. 'We won't be able to try that out here, will we? You can bet your socks no banana's going to have a chance to get over-ripe with you around.'

ONLY US CHICKENS

I always thought of the remainder of my childhood as growing up in the real world. A thing called the depression had happened by the time we moved to Brighton, and there was a lot of talk about why it had occurred, and how it could be overcome. We certainly had much less money, and so did thousands of other people.

We only had one maid, and my mother, being a trained nurse, helped my father in the surgery when he needed her. The surgery and waiting room weren't separated from the rest of the house, so patients were often found wandering down the back hall, looking for the bathroom, or they walked into the sitting room by mistake. Once when some school friends and I were singing around the pianola, a strange baritone voice joined in. It was my turn to pump the pedals, and when I looked around there was a patient I recognised by sight, singing 'A Wandering Minstrel, I' with great enthusiasm. He enjoyed it so much he forgot about the time, and my father was a bit put out when he thought he had finished the evening surgery about nine o'clock, and this man came out of the sitting room where he had been giving us a solo of 'The Barcarole'.

In those days there were private patients and Lodge patients, who got all their medical attention for one guinea a year. My father took on a good many Lodge patients to build up his practice, and my mother became a bit upset at times because some of them came in every week to see him.

'That Mr Ostler's here again,' she would announce to my father as he ate his lunch after his morning round. 'He's holding forth to the whole waiting room, which is packed, by the way. But don't hurry your lunch Toby, you'll get indigestion.'

'He's a lonely man since his wife died,' my father would reply. 'He knows he has to wait until the end, after the more

111

urgent cases. Besides, you know you like the pots of marmalade he brings us.'

At first my mother found it hard to get used to having the patients invading our private lives like this, but gradually her curiosity and her natural love of people got the better of her, and if I couldn't find her after school I would try the waiting room, and there she would be, copying down Mr Ostler's recipes for strawberry jam and marmalade.

Sometimes the patients forgot she was in there, and one day she came out full of indignation, because one of the patients had said to another: 'Oh, don't bother about your bill if you're hard up. Dr Giblin's easy.'

In fact, he sometimes lent the patients money if he could see they were unemployed, and with no food in the house for their children. He worried too about the other sort of Lodge patients — the ones who didn't like to call him in too often because they paid so little, and were often very ill before he saw them.

My mother scolded him for being soft, but only in a half-hearted fashion, because she was soft herself, and always bought shoelaces and combs from the tired-looking returned servicemen who had had to resort to door-to-door selling to try to make a living.

My mother's real weakness was stray dogs and cats. Everyone in the district knew that she wouldn't turn an animal away, so they popped kittens over our fence and pushed stray dogs through our gate. Beside our own two cockers and two or three cats, we nearly always had a stray or two. Because my mother had the gift of the gab, she used to talk people into giving homes to some very odd-looking cross-breeds.

I can see her now, talking into the black telephone which hung on the wall in the back hall, stroking with one foot a large, strange-looking shaggy dog.

'Ah, he's a beauty' she is telling the patient, who, my father reports, has lost his old dog and is thinking about getting another. 'He's *almost* a cocker spaniel, and he has the most beautiful brown eyes.'

The dog rolls over and waves his paws in the air, trying to please her by looking as much like a cocker as possible. I can remember that in this case, the dog, by his sheer devotion to my mother, ended up by staying with us, and seemed to grow another foot taller. Fortunately, in those days it was very cheap to feed animals — the butcher gave you a big newspaper parcel of meat scraps and bones free, if you bought other meat from him.

The one thing my mother really objected to in our new life was only having one bathroom, and having to allow the patients to use our lavatory at times. ('Never refer to it as "a toilet",' she told us. 'It's vulgar.')

When she complained about the bathroom to my father, he remarked: 'Well, there's always the one out in the stables in an emergency.' It was a wonderful refuge actually, with a long wooden seat, and it was so private in that part of the garden that you could leave the door open and watch the white Leghorns and Buff Orpingtons scratching around in their yard.

'What! And share it with the gardener!' my mother exclaimed when he mentioned it.

'Well, you couldn't really. It's not a two-holer.'

This was the rudest thing I can ever remember my father saying. My mother was really taken aback for a moment, then she couldn't help laughing. My father was very fond of jokes, but they were always what Bubba and I privately called 'corny' as we grew up. He never told jokes about sex, because he didn't think it was amusing. He was a very romantic man, who wrote songs with sentimental lyrics. Sometimes he dashed out in the middle of surgery to try out a new tune that had come into his head, on the piano. I don't think he should really have been a doctor, although he was a very dedicated one. One of his patients gave him a book of jokes once, and he was delighted. He hid it away, and doled out the jokes to us, two or three a day. The standard of jokes in the book wasn't exactly high, as you can see if I tell you his favourite joke in the book. I know it off by heart:

'A man was passing his fowlhouse by night when he thought he heard a disturbance.

' "Is anyone there?" he asked, and a gruff voice replied:

' "No, only us chickens." '

Well.

For years afterwards Bubba could always reduce me nearly to hysterics by saying in a gruff voice (which she did very well): 'No, only us chickens.'

KNIGHT ERRANT

The best part of the long wooden building in our back garden at Brighton was the hayloft, and this was so dilapidated that Bubba and I were forbidden to go up there. My father said the ladder and the floor of the loft were both unsafe, and this naturally made it irresistible to us. It was very tall, so with the door open you could see out for miles. I always thought I could see the sea two miles away, but I think it was really just the edge of the sky, shimmering.

I spent many hours lying on the floor of the loft, reading, and chewing aniseed squares. (Also forbidden. It was hard to get your teeth clean before dinner.) It was wonderfully peaceful with the smell of old hay tickling my nostrils, and the squeaking and scuttering of mice sounding in my ears. The abundance of mice made the loft a mecca for stray cats, of which there seemed to be prodigious numbers in those long ago days before animals were spayed and neutered.

I found two kittens up there once, no larger than mice themselves, and with no sign of a mother. When I took up milk and an eyedropper which I had borrowed from the surgery, they were ravenous, so next day I took them down the rickety ladder, one by one, inside my jumper which I tucked in my pants.

It was a heart-stopping enterprise, as the ladder looked like a mouth with half the teeth missing and the rest rotten, and the kittens were wild and scared and scratched at me desperately. They were tiny though, and weak, and their hissing was no louder than spats of water falling from a kettle into a hot stove.

My parents weren't very enthusiastic about them, my father saying they looked rickety and mangy, but they finally ended up in a basket in a warm corner of the kitchen.

My father was right as usual. The kittens had ringworm, which Bubba and I caught — inevitable as we had each taken a kitten to bed. The treatment in those days involved having our heads shaved, and staying away from school until we were better. When we did go back, we had to wear calico mob caps which certainly didn't improve our image.

The kittens fared better — they had to be shaved too, and painted purple in patches, but they looked quite quaint. It was quite a long while before they were allowed back into the house though.

I couldn't help feeling it wasn't much good doing kind deeds if that sort of thing happened. I had just started being accepted into the group of girls I admired, and now they were drawing away as if I had the plague. It was weeks before they really accepted me again.

Although my father was always talking about having the stables pulled down, it wasn't even done after this disastrous episode. It proved to be too costly to replace them with a brick garage — there was never enough spare money to start on the project. Then the war came, and nobody even thought about it for years, but about ten years later history repeated itself. My father parked his car in the stables, which now looked as if they should have a danger sign of them, and came inside saying he could hear kittens mewing in the loft. They peered out the doorway when we went outside, mewing piteously. There was no question of climbing the rickety stairs any longer, we decided, so we aimed pieces of meat at the doorway and wondered where we could borrow a very long ladder. My mother said of course the fire brigade would come, they were always rescuing animals. One or two of them were patients and they were lovely men.

Fortunately, while I was wondering if it would be all right to call them, a man I had recently met came to see me. I was delighted, and explained that he had called at just the right moment. I asked if he would mind rescuing the kittens, and he said 'of course', without blinking an eyelid, the darling man.

The kittens were older than the ones I had rescued years ago, and considerably wilder, but in the end he managed to lower them down in a sugar bag, but not without damaging himself in the process. I hadn't realised he was allergic to cats, and his hands and neck came up in a lattice-work of weals where they had scratched him. I used up all the samples of anti-histamine cream in the surgery on them, although he kept telling me not to fuss.

The kittens were so wild that we had to let them live outside, feeding them enormously so that they didn't kill the birds. They lurked around in the undergrowth for years, two lean grey shadows.

Their rescuer came around to see me the next evening to find out how they were getting on. I thought this was so sweet of him after the scratches they had inflicted, that I made up my mind immediately to marry him if he asked me.

When I told my husband today that I had written an account of his rescue of the kittens, and called it 'Knight Errant' he was horrified.

'How embarrassing. Please don't put it in,' he said.

But I couldn't resist.

Moira with a litter of kittens from the loft, 1935.

TRUE LOVERS' KNOTS

When we went to live at Brighton, it was the end of having maids and governesses and nannies and so on. There was a thing called 'the depression' which meant, my father said, that nobody had much money at all.

Bubba and I liked it better, because we went to a real school, and at home we had Linda.

Linda was our household help, a country girl my mother had found through advertising in *The Leader* for a cook general. She got lots of telephone calls, because there were dozens of country girls during the depression, without jobs, who were dying to get down to the city and a live-in job. Fortunately, we were lucky. Linda was the first girl who rang up, and my mother engaged her without an interview because she liked her voice on the telephone. Linda, my mother declared a week after she had started, was a treasure, because her roast potatoes were always crisp, and because she wasn't flighty.

We had the feeling, though, that because of her good manners and attractive speaking voice, Linda could have got away with soggy potatoes and a wild flirtation with the ice man. I mention the ice man, although there were several other tradesmen who delivered, like the grocer (a free bag of boiled sweets thrown in) and the baker ('I hope I'm in time for the doctor's lunch?') but it was the ice man who took such a fancy to Linda. I didn't blame him. I thought Linda was lovely, with her shining brown hair, cut in a fringe, her pink cheeks, and her pretty print dresses with their neat Peter Pan collars. The ice man, who was large and black-haired, would come into the kitchen carrying a great block of ice on a piece of sacking on his shoulder. When he had chipped away at it with his ice pick, to make it fit into the top of the icebox, he would stand in the kitchen doorway and try to talk to Linda, the lethal looking ice pick dangling from one big hand, the piece of sacking dripping from the other. Linda would look at the puddle forming on the old green and black patterned linoleum, and twist her engagement ring with its one small diamond. (Surely he would take the hint?)

Linda was engaged to be married to a farmer from her home town, but he was a younger son, and it would be some time before he and Linda managed to save up enough money for a property of their own.

The ice man just pretended not to understand when Linda mentioned her fiancé — I think he was too besotted about Linda to care. When he was in the kitchen there was a strange atmosphere there — a sort of hot, brooding feeling. I tried to explain about this to Linda, and she got the giggles and couldn't stop. I wished she would, because I knew she would start me off too, and that was one thing my mother really objected to. She said it was fine to have a good laugh about things, but giggling was vulgar.

Finally Linda managed to say: 'You'd think all that ice would damp down the hot brooding feeling.'

This started me off too, and I ended up with hiccups, which was always a give-away. My mother looked at me suspiciously when I went into the dining room, and said: 'What's been going on out there?'

I decided I had better explain about the ice man, and my mother said that if he was worrying Linda, she or my father would speak to him, or, easier still and less embarrassing, Linda was to stay out of the kitchen when he came, and I could give him his shilling if my mother wasn't around.

He came very early in the morning, so I was generally cleaning out my love bird aviary, blowing the husks off the panicum seed, and giving them fresh water. The original pair of yellow and green love birds had luckily proved to be a good breeding couple, and I now had about a dozen young ones. It was easy to see why they were called love birds.

One morning the ice man arrived while I was inside the aviary, so I told him to wait just a moment and I would come in and get his money. He admired the love birds, and said he'd often thought of getting a pair, and I wondered if I should offer him a couple as a sort of consolation prize, but I remembered my mother had said not to encourage him in any way. I felt sorry for him though, standing there with the big block of ice balanced on his shoulder, dripping down his shirt, but it was time he stopped having any false hopes.

'Where's Linda?' he asked as usual.

'In her room, finishing a letter to her fiancé. She wants to catch the mail,' I said firmly.

'You think she's really keen on him?' he asked, getting very red around the ears.

'Terribly,' I said, because there was no use trying to let him down lightly.

A few weeks later a new ice man appeared — a large middle-aged man who wasn't very good at first at trying to hack bits off the blocks to make them fit.

'Where's Jack?' Linda asked.

'Joined the Navy, just like that,' said the new man cheerfully.

It should have been a great relief to Linda, but she gave a big sigh. I knew what she meant — Jack had been a worry, but at the same time he had added a bit of drama to her boring life, and I suppose it's always flattering if someone seems to be mad about you.

Linda spent all her spare time preparing her glory box. I became very involved in this project, and Linda taught me new fancywork stitches so that I could help her embroider the countless doilies, tablecloths and tea towels she was storing away in her camphorwood chest. Every now and then, they would be taken out and washed and ironed to 'freshen them up', and Linda would lay them out on her bed to gloat over them. Linda and I often went to the haberdashery shop up the street to choose new articles to embroider. The trouble was, Linda had been engaged for two years, and she had such a collection of linen now that she was getting what she called 'choosey'.

'I'm sick and tired of ladies in bonnets and cottages and gardens,' she confessed to the owner of the shop. 'I've got enough bluebirds too, and as for kittens and puppies... no, I think I'll just give up.'

Realising that she was going to lose a valued customer, the draper suggested that Linda could be more artistic if she bought some good quality linen and ironed transfers on it to make her own designs.

'You could mix several transfers — it makes you more creative — like painting a picture, almost,' she explained. Linda liked the idea immediately, and chose several transfers of true lovers' knots and plenty of bright blue silk to embroider her sets of white and pale pink underwear.

I spent all my pocket money on butterflies. It was wonderful ironing them onto a piece of white linen. The warm iron smelled comforting, and I got so carried away that I used all the butter-flies on one piece of material, which Linda thought was a bit extravagant.

Bubba didn't take part in these feminine pursuits. She was too busy pulling up her baby carrots to measure them and re-planting them carefully in the same holes. She was also practis-ing for the school sports, which were going to be a most exciting event in our lives. Bubba was doing very well in the practice races, and had borrowed a china egg from our hens and one of the best silver spoons, because the egg fitted into it more tightly than it did in the kitchen spoon. She also came in to dinner covered with flakes of bran, because she used an old chook-food sack to practise for the sack race. She did however take time off to look at Linda's trousseau when it was laid out on the bed, and gave her advice about which she liked.

She was very taken with a tea towel embroidered with two fat kittens in a yellow basket. She was less polite about the sets of underwear with true lovers' knots embroidered in smooth blue satin stitch, and little rosebuds scattered artistically around them.

'It's a waste of time, Linda,' Bubba explained. 'I'd do more tea towels if I were you. Nobody ever sees your pants.'

Linda, blushing, kept sewing furiously as if her life depended on it.

THE DYING SWAN

I was very short of grandparents as a child. I only had one — my paternal grandmother — and perhaps because of this I felt very close to her once we came over to live on the mainland. My mother's parents, who were Irish, had died before I was born, and my Tasmanian grandfather had died before even my father was born. I kept wondering how this could be true. I felt it quite incomprehensible that this could have happened, because in those early days I had no realisation that conception takes place nine months before birth.

My grandfather, a young solicitor of thirty-one, was riding along a mountain trail on a horse, which slipped and fell on him. He died a week later of peritonitis. I have always been led to believe by my father that it was on Mount Wellington that this accident occurred, so that as a child the blue shadow of that mountain seemed to loom over me like a livid bruise. It is there in the background of the lives of everyone who lives in Hobart of course, but I felt a certain dread of it rather than just an awareness of its shape, which changed from slate colour to navy blue, and altered the mood of the whole town nestling at its foot. When my great-uncle wrote a family history which stated that it was on a trip to Mount Zeehan to inspect the mining prospects there that my grandfather was injured, I felt quite bewildered and disoriented. I had invested Mount Wellington with a menace which hadn't existed. It was not, after all, the evil mountain of a Grimm's fairytale. On picnics on the way up the mountain, I had resisted becoming bewitched by its ferny gullies, by its magical purplish blue drymophila berries on their fragile stems. I told it that it had killed my grandfather and made my grandmother look pale and sad. Even my father looked sad when he spoke of Gran, and her lonely life.

Wherever this old tragedy had occurred, it had altered the

course of many lives forever. My grandmother, who already had two small daughters, became very ill, and it was feared she would lose the baby she was carrying, but six months later my father was born. My grandmother, gentle, blue-eyed and with the whitest skin I can ever remember seeing, numbly and unprotestingly allowed Grandma Giblin to organise their lives.

I wish I had known Great-Grandma Giblin. There is a marvellous painting of her, as Mary Ann Worthy, aged about eighteen, done by the poisoner Wainwright. My great-uncle tells the story of a first painting being rejected, because Mary Ann was holding her head at an angle which was not a natural one for her. In the second highly successful attempt, she appears to be flashing her blue eyes at the painter in an indignant manner, which gives her the spirited appearance that was typical of her.

According to my great-uncle, it appears as if she was thinking: 'How dare you, a convict, address me in this way.'

Whatever her reactions at this stage, she was a most kind and philanthropic woman, stepmother to four children when she was only nineteen, and mother to eight more.

Taking control of my father's family was just one small addition to the numerous calls on her time and resources. Luckily there were plenty of servants to help with the sad widow, the sickly little baby boy and the two bewildered little girls.

In spite of numerous admirers who came and worshipped from a distance — a very considerable distance, having a healthy respect for great-grand-mama — my own grandmother never re-married. Neither did she toil and spin, because firstly she was looked after by an army of servants, and later the elder daughter turned down proposals of marriage in order to look after her mother. A sad waste really of two lives which could have been so much richer and more rewarding. Instead, my grandmother played the piano hour after hour, the clear pure notes spilling out into the garden where the children played with their nurse. The pieces she played were always sad, my father used to tell me. She played so well that she was asked by a world-famous violinist who visited Hobart if she would become

126

his accompanist, and travel around the world with him, but Grandma Giblin sternly forbade this. To play for money? How vulgar! How unthinkable! Besides, there were the children to be considered, and I don't think for one minute that my grandmother seriously considered the idea herself. It was just flattering to be asked, and made a good story for the family memoirs.

When we came to live in Melbourne, we visited grandmother and Aunt Marjorie in various apartments in old houses in Armadale, where we sat indoors on Sunday afternoons while Gran played the piano and Aunt Marjorie accompanied her on the violin. The wailing sadness of the violin always affected me like the screech of chalk on a blackboard, so I concentrated instead on the many old photographs in their heavy silver frames. Most of these were of a slender young man with a small moustache. Her husband, the first Arthur Leslie. There is one photograph I have of them both still, my grandfather standing beside her chair, where she sat, eyes huge in a small triangular face, a small secret smile on her lips, forever frozen in the eternal youth of their marriage.

I became closest to my grandmother when I was in my late teens, and was experiencing the heady excitements and black despairs of first love. I realised at last what a desolate waste her life had been since the age of twenty-three. She would have been better off also without an army of servants to separate her from her children in the early years. If she had had to look after them, to ensure their survival even, it would have kept her closer to the warm mainstream of life, instead of inhabiting an unreal, unhappy dream world. But she must have had happy memories of that happy long-ago marriage still, because I found her very easy to talk to.

'Tell me about your latest young man, darling,' she would say, seated inevitably at her piano even when she wasn't playing. As I spoke she would pick out a few notes, idly, softly, then maybe improvise them into a theme as a background for what I was saying.

When I was seventeen I remember visiting her on my way

home from Melbourne University, where I had started an Arts degree. I needed to tell her about my new love, the one I was sure at the moment was going to be my last love, there would never be another.

Gran sat at her piano, dressed in her favourite colour, a dull slate blue, with several chiffon scarves draped around her neck. Her white hair was piled on top of her head, secured with tortoiseshell combs.

'Tell me all about him dear,' she murmured on this occasion, my poor Aunt Marjorie having been banished to the kitchenette to make a cup of tea.

She started playing one of her favourite pieces, 'The Dying Swan', her thin white hands, stiffened now with age, still managing to coax magical sound from the keys. It was somehow easy to confide in her, with the music rippling out softly as a background, and I was often surprised, as on this occasion, by the length of time that went by.

'And when he sits opposite me in the library, Gran, while we are studying, it gives me the most peculiar feeling when he suddenly looks up and smiles at me. Do you think it's love?'

She inclined her head, without speaking, to imply that indeed she did. It was then that I noticed, glancing down at her hands, which had come to rest, 'The Dying Swan' finished, that there were two tears glistening on their backs, rolling off slowly onto the yellow ivory keys.

THE GOLD CUP

My father's elder sister Marjorie was a handsome woman, as I remember her during the latter part of her life, with abundant white hair, piled up in a sort of beehive, anchored with several tortoiseshell combs which she stuck into it in a haphazard fashion. She had a pink and white complexion which she had always guarded from the sun, and the same intensely blue eyes as my father. I thought of her as handsome rather than beautiful because her aquiline nose became pronounced in later life, and also because there was a lack of something in her expression — a lack of living, perhaps. Certainly, in the many tinted photographs that remain of Aunt Marjorie in her youth, she was very beautiful as a young woman, with her piled up black hair. She was often photographed holding a single red rose, an enigmatic smile on her lips.

Born in 1884 in Hobart, by the time she was three the pattern of her life had been set. Her father had died in 1887 after a fall from a horse, leaving his young widow with two small girls and another baby due to be born. That baby — my father — arrived six months after his father's death.

Great-grandma Giblin helped with the young family, and there seemed to be no lack of money or servants. My grandmother never re-married, although there are reports of several suitors. Whether my grandmother remained a widow because she had no heart for another marriage, or because Grandma Giblin was a strict chaperone, no one will ever know. So Aunt Marjorie, in spite of numerous admirers, and a couple of engagements, never married. She was the daughter who stayed at home and devoted her life to mother, who had sunk gently back into a life of mourning.

All that remains of Aunt Marjorie's lovers are various slim volumes of poetry, beautifully bound, ranging from the *Sonnets of Shakespeare*, encompassing Browning's poems, and even including such weighty topics as Lord Macaulay's *Lays of Ancient Rome*. This offering, tastefully bound in dark green leather and gold, does not appear to have been much read. It is inscribed 'To dearest Marjorie, from her most devoted admirer, C.E.'

At one stage Aunt Marjorie was secretly engaged to a young Swedish man with a double-barrelled name who ran a gymnasium, but my grandmother managed to persuade her that it 'wasn't quite the thing' to become the wife of somebody who taught physical culture. Looking back, it is hard to determine whether Aunt Marjorie discarded her suitors because of Gran's rather selfish possessiveness, or because Marjorie herself had not a strong enough inclination towards marriage.

Certainly she was devoted to her mother, and they lived together in a series of apartments in elegant but decaying houses in Armadale and Malvern. There was a sameness and a shabbiness about these apartments which was terribly depressing to me as a child. They were all in two-storey Victorian houses owned by impoverished widows. There was always one elegant room with long windows, where Gran's piano would be installed so that she could look out on the garden as she played. Sometimes the wallpaper would be damp and stained, but there would somehow be an air of faded grandeur, a hint of past glories in this room where visitors were received. Inevitably the rest of the apartment would be shabby: a reasonable bedroom, generally a shared bathroom, and a small makeshift kitchen, partitioned off and smelling of gas.

'Queen Anne in front and Mary Ann behind,' my mother used to say afterwards when we had visited them in yet another apartment. It worried her that they could have obtained something far more comfortable for the same rent, but they were determined to stay within the same small and rather expensive area. It was important to them to be close to their church, and their friends who came for afternoon tea. Above all, it was important to 'keep up appearances'.

When Gran died Aunt Marjorie was quite lost. With no career, and no hobbies other than her music, she had little to occupy her. My sister and I visited her alternately on Saturdays for what she called 'an *al fresco* lunch'. It was served on the lap — Aunt Marjorie had invented eating from trays long before the advent of TV — and it generally consisted of Welsh rarebit and a rich chocolate mousse. We had what she called 'a cosy chat', and invariably when I left she whispered in my ear that I was her favourite niece, and she was going to leave me a gold cup in her will.

This went on for years, and although I didn't feel acquisitive about this mysterious cup, I decided one day that it would be polite to take an interest in it. I asked where she kept it, and whether I could see it. I thought perhaps it might even be a figment of her imagination.

Aunt Marjorie replied in a hushed voice that it was far too valuable to keep in her flat, and was at her bank with her will. Poor Aunt Marjorie, with so little to leave anyone, was forever going off to her solicitor to alter her will.

The years passed. When my mother died, and my father was left in a large house with a housekeeper, Aunt Marjorie finally decided to go and live with him. My father, although he had offered her a home for years, was rather alarmed by the thought of Aunt Marjorie permanently under his roof. She had become extremely talkative in her old age — my mother called it 'the gift of the gab', but my father, in brotherly fashion, complained that 'Marjorie would talk the hind leg off a horse.'

However, the problem solved itself, because Aunt Marjorie ensconced herself in the waiting room during consulting hours, and talked to the patients. They were mostly elderly people who had been coming for years, and were quite happy for Aunt Marjorie to tell them what a wonderful doctor her brother was, or to reminisce about his sporting prowess at Geelong Grammar and the university, and his wartime experiences.

'So nice that he became a captain. An officer and a gentle-man.' I can hear her saying it now, and therein, I realise, lies the central truth of Aunt Marjorie's life. She was, because of the way she had been brought up, an incredible snob. She spoke to me at times about her past loves, and that was her highest praise of them. 'He was such a gentleman dear.' And sometimes she would add vaguely: '*Noblesse oblige*'. I didn't know what this meant the first time she said it, and looked it up in my dictionary: 'Benevolent and honourable behaviour considered to be the responsibility of people of high birth' it said. Help! I thought.

Aunt Marjorie died of a heart attack at the age of eighty, and in due course her solicitor asked me to call and collect a little memento she had left me. I had three children by then, and Aunt Marjorie had left our second daughter, Amanda, twenty-five pounds to buy a pony. Amanda, when she was about nine, was a warm-hearted little girl who listened to Aunt Marjorie for hours. At this age she had badly wanted a pony, but by the time Aunt Marjorie died, Amanda had discovered boys and forgotten about ponies, and the equivalent of twenty-five pounds wouldn't procure one anyway, so we had to cheat on that a bit.

My memento was of course the gold cup, which proved to be indeed gold. A yellow china cup and saucer, with gold leaf on the handle and around the rim. It has a delicate and charming picture of five nymphs painted on it, and is probably quite valuable.

When my sister called in, I took her into the sitting room and showed her the elegant little cup sitting on the mantelpiece.

'Look, I've collected Aunt Marj's cup,' I said, and watched her face register surprise and then amusement.

'That's what she promised *me*. She said I was her favourite niece,' she replied. We both started to laugh.

But, as we sobered up again, we realised it was sad rather than funny. Poor Aunt Marjorie, who had ended her life with one treasured possession, and who had promised it to both of us, perhaps in the hope that we would visit her more often if each of us thought we were the favourite niece.

THE TRUNK

From the earliest times, once I had mastered the rudiments of forming the letters and the words, I needed to write. I filled threepenny exercise book after threepenny exercise book, until I prevailed upon my father to pass on to me the large medical diaries which were given to general practitioners by pharmaceutical companies in those days.

I kept a sort of diary or journal in which I wrote not only the daily happenings of my life, but also thoughts and ideas that came to me. I copied out, too, any passages from poets and writers which particularly appealed to me. I also had a suitcase full of stories and poems under my bed.

Fortunately, by the time I was sixteen, I had a wonderful English mistress for my Leaving Honours year at school. She persuaded me to start doing something with all this material I had garnered. On my seventeenth birthday, just before I left school, my parents gave me a small portable typewriter. I was completely overcome and elated. Nobody I knew had a typewriter in those days, and I thought it made me an author overnight.

I didn't realise that the words that came so trippingly from the tongue didn't just trip lightly from this infernal little machine. I persevered, first with one finger, and as there was no erasing key, nor had I ever heard of whiting out liquid, the results were lamentable.

I thought they looked wonderful though, and started sending them off under a pen-name to women's magazines and the supplements of newspapers. And they sold, maybe because I had so much confidence. Finally the editor of a weekend supplement rang and said he was publishing a story and had I any more. He said my pen name — which was Blair Lane — sounded like something out of a street directory, and I had to be brave enough to publish under my own name. I refused, but he knew what he was about, this editor, and he rang a few days later to say he could only publish the latest story I had sent him under my real name, as it wasn't their policy to allow any one author too many acceptances. As a penurious university student, I agreed. The result was that some of my father's patients told him they found it a bit odd that a girl of my age had written this story about a near rape, and lots of pent-up emotions. (I re-read it the other day, and found it very funny.) But I could see that even my father was a bit shaken, although I kept reassuring him that it wasn't written from personal experience.

Apart from this rather trivial stuff, I had started on a novel, which was far more serious but it only came to me at odd times in small flashes.

By the end of 1941 the war seemed to be closing in around us. I decided to defer the remainder of my Arts course. There were too many ghosts wandering the cloisters at the university.

I ended up in the Navy Code and Cipher room for four years, which, alternately boring and exciting, drained all my energy, especially on the midnight watch. We worked on our codes and cyphers under blue fluorescent lights which made us look ghastly — green and hollow-eyed. The worst hour of the night was before the dawn; before the sun started to light up the Shrine and the air-raid shelters across the road. Nurses tell you that there is a certain low ebb of energy about that time, when death is more apt to come. It applies too, I'm sure, to a feeling one gets about then — a time to reach some core within us, the soul, call it what you will. It is the hour when the lieutenants I worked with took a few minutes off for a cup of coffee, and started to bare their souls, to confess that their girlfriends or fiancées had left them for somebody else — generally an American serviceman — or that their wives didn't understand them. Men who normally never made a single personal remark unburdened themselves as if it was a relief to get things off their minds. There was nothing you could do, except offer them tea and sympathy and one of your rationed cigarettes — a whole pack of ten out of your thirty a week ration if you felt sorry enough.

It was marvellous material though. I wrote far more on the midnight watch than on the other two shifts, partly because I heard so many sad variations on the same theme. Sometimes I wrote to shut out the messages we had de-coded the night before — I never got over being upset if we received a message from a sinking ship, or if a coast-watcher let us know he was burning his cipher books because he knew the Japanese were closing in on his island.

I had written several hundred pages of a novel by this time, even if the going was slow, sitting there heavy-eyed, fingering my dead meat tickets. Those awful identity discs — the colour of liver, with our I.D. numbers and religions on them — a constant reminder of a war that never came as far south as Melbourne. I really expected it to, once the midget submarines reached Sydney Harbour, but I was obviously becoming a pessimist by then.

I can't remember anything very special about the end of the war — just lots and lots of torn-up paper being thrown out the windows at the Barracks. It was an anti-climax too because our jobs went on for quite a while, mine until a kindly doctor gave me a certificate saying I needed to be put out to grass — like a broken-down race horse! How I disliked him. It gave me more time to write, though.

A couple of years later, I married the man who had rescued the kittens. The newspaper editor who was still publishing my work if I produced any, asked me to call in and see him. He wanted to give me a pep talk, I think, about getting on with my writing. Instead, I waved my engagement ring at him and told him I was getting married.

He was horrified.

'Don't!' he said. 'You are just getting there. Put it off. Postpone it. Gestation will take over.'

I thought he'd gone mad, and told him so in no uncertain

terms.

'I've nearly finished my novel. Nothing will stop me now. I have nearly enough material to divide it in half.' And I had too. Literally a hundredweight or so of it.

Time went by, and he was proved right, because I was too absorbed in my husband, and later my two small daughters as well, to bother to write. Every now and then something occurred to me that was so compelling that I had to write it down, but all that I really needed to do now was to make a final draft of my novel.

We always seemed to live in houses that were a little too small for us. When we moved to Brighton I stored all my note-books, all my published stories, all my university notes, and my novel, in an old wooden trunk which had belonged to my husband's great-grandfather back in his ship-building days in Hobart. It was made of wood, and covered with leather which had rotted over the years. It had metal corners, but no locks.

I was just deciding I must get this novel tidied up and sent off, when I had another baby, after six years. The day our son was born my husband bought a bigger house, and even this was a little small for all the junk we had accumulated over the years. But it had a big play-house in the back garden, and that was where we stored the excess furniture, the rocking-horse, the pusher and... the trunk.

At various times during the next twelve months my husband said he was worried about all the things in the play-house, and that it would be good for the girls to be able to use it. He wanted me to sort through everything with him. But I was tired, and I enjoyed playing with the baby and watching the girls relate to their small brother. I kept putting off the shed, and I buried the thought of the novel, which nagged at me now and again.

Finally my husband decided to make a start on the junk, and he lit the incinerator. You may not have heard of them — I think they are banned these days, and rightfully so. We went through a certain amount of old belongings — a depressing thing to do as in some cases the moths had got there first. Then, he carefully hosed down the incinerator, and that, we thought, was the end of it.

Next evening at six-thirty, I was feeding the baby, keeping an eye on the lamb chops, and trying to supervise my younger daughter's bath which was almost over the top. There was a loud peal at the front door bell, and as my husband was on the telephone I answered it.

I was confronted by an agitated young man, who started off: 'Pardon me for taking the liberty of intruding on your privacy...' Help, Jehovah's Witnesses, I thought, forgetting they always travel in pairs.

'Sorry... too busy' I said firmly, trying to close the door, but he persevered: '*But...* there is rather a large fire in your back garden.'

Large fire! When I put my head over the verandah railing a wall of flame was leaping up behind the garage.

When my husband had rung the fire brigade he dashed out to rescue the cars from the garage, saying if the petrol exploded our house and the neighbour's could catch alight.

It was a spectacular fire, and it stopped the traffic for miles. It had its funny moments. I remember hearing somebody hacking their way through the side fence, which was nearly new.

'It's all right, Jim,' I called out to the neighbour. 'The fire brigade will be here in a minute.' Then a man wearing a brass helmet leapt through the hole he had just made, just like Superman, and said: 'Madam, I *am* the fire brigade.' I hadn't realised they crashed their way through to your property from the nearest fire hydrant, which is a very effective way to cope with things.

By midnight all was calm. The children were asleep, our elder daughter pacified with a note saying why she hadn't been able to do her homework. The neighbours, fortified with drinks, had departed.

'Oh, my God,' said my husband suddenly. 'Your trunk! All your writing — I'll go and search.' But he knew, as I did, that it had been completely consumed. I had watched the firemen rake over the ashes, and seen the twisted metal strips that had bound it.

I made light of it, saying the novel had been weighing me down, I knew I would never have finished it. I could see he blamed himself, but who would imagine that a fire could travel underground, among the roots of the buffalo grass, and flare up a day later?

We realised next day that we could claim insurance on the playhouse, and in due course the inspector came out to assess the damage. After he had measured the site, we went inside to work out the contents of the shed. I asked him if he would like a cup of coffee, then, eyeing his nose, which would have done credit to the Dong with the Luminous Nose, I asked him if he would prefer a whisky. Although it was only eleven in the morning, he settled down with half a bottle of Scotch and proceeded to make a list of toys, suitcases, and so on, allowing what seemed a very generous amount for each. At the end he asked:

'Are you sure there's nothing else? People often forget some items until it's too late.' He was re-filling his glass as he spoke, and filling in time. There was still some Scotch left in the bottle.

I hesitated. I hadn't wanted to mention the trunk. 'Just an old trunk, with personal papers in it. Stories I had written, diaries and notes. Of intrinsic value to me, but...'

'I'm afraid there's nothing we can do about that. What a shame...' Then his face brightened.

'But the trunk! Old trunks are very much in demand these days. Say I allow you fifty pounds on the trunk?'

RETURN TO SENDER

I went into the city last week for the first time in a year. When I had finished my shopping and walked to the bus stop, I found I had been foolish to break my rule of always shopping in the suburbs. There had been a bomb scare, and all the buses had been diverted away from the city. There were police cars with flashing yellow lights, and people were standing around in great huddled lumps.

There was a long queue waiting for the bus, and people started to talk to each other. Everyone wanted to know where the bomb was supposed to be, and a very important woman in a purple raincoat said it was near Nicholson Street, she had been forced to get off her tram there earlier, and had been ferried into the city by bus.

'Ah, just near the Russell Street police station,' a man near me said, and the information was passed through the crowd. It was like that game of 'Secrets' we played as children, when the message became distorted as it was whispered breathily, and with fits of giggles. Except that this wasn't funny, and the crowd was apprehensive, and restless.

There were two sharp explosions close by, and I could smell gunpowder. Before we had time to panic, two policemen grabbed a young boy who had been letting off fire-crackers and didn't know any better than to make such a noise during a bomb alert.

A woman near me said, 'What is happening to us all, Holy Angel of God?' She had an Irish accent, and it took me right back to my childhood in Hobart. I found I was standing in the middle of an alien uneasy crowd, repeating a prayer I hadn't said for half a century:

> *Angel of God, my guardian dear*
> *To whom his love commits me here.*

Ever this day be at my side
To light and guard, to rule and guide. Amen

Perhaps I spoke aloud, because a small woman in a neat grey suit touched my arm, and asked if I could help her. She said she hadn't long been out of hospital, and was beginning to feel faint. I asked someone who had managed to get a seat at the bus stop if they would allow her to sit down, and I tried to find a taxi, but not one came along during our long wait.

When the bus finally arrived, we sat together. I thought longingly of the new paperback in my bag as we continued to talk.

The woman wore beautiful black suede gloves, which made me feel nostalgic. They were the sort my mother used to buy on shopping trips to George's.

We talked of the odd weather, the younger generation, the Bomb. She thought the Bomb was to blame both for the weather and the indifference and violence of the young, who felt its shadow over their future. I answered vaguely. It was the sort of conversation one had so often these days.

The bus stopped to pick up some passengers outside a house which had a huge weeping willow in its front garden. Raindrops from an earlier shower still glistened on the leaves, intensifying the piercingly tender green. The branches swayed like slender chains of shimmering tears. Like frozen, icy tears.

It was so beautiful it made my throat constrict. I turned to my companion to point out its delicate tracery against the clearing sky. It was then I noticed there were tears running down her cheeks, a river un-dammed. She told me how much it meant to her to see a thing of such beauty as the willow, as she had been blinded a year ago by a brain tumour, and had recently regained her sight after some delicate neuro-surgery.

She was a brave and intelligent woman, sitting quietly with her hands folded in her lap in their black suede gloves. With tears still running unchecked down her face, she explained to me that she didn't know how permanent the recovery of her sight would be. She was sewing buttons on all her husband's shirts, and buying up a supply of clothes for him, as well as feasting her eyes on every beautiful thing she saw, etching it into her memory against the possible darkness of the future.

She told me the surgeon had started the operation through the roof of her mouth, but she had haemorrhaged so much he had to continue it through her temple. I glanced surreptitiously at her forehead, but could see no scar. It was apparently hidden by the neat grey hair which curved forward around her face. She told me about the chemotherapy she had since undergone at the Peter McCallum clinic, and how she imagined each time she had been through the atomic bomb fall out, and identified with the people of Chernobyl.

When I reached home I felt restless and unhappy, as if the woman had touched off an old grief, only half remembered. I walked the floor, cradling a mug of coffee in my hands to warm them, trying to pin down this elusive feeling. Later, sitting at my desk, I noticed the *Rubaiyat*, and it came back to me. I had never associated Brian with the weeping willow before, but I thought of him whenever anyone quoted Omar Khayyam.

It was all so long ago. I was sixteen, almost seventeen, and looking forward to starting an Arts degree at Melbourne University in a few weeks' time. The war had started, but it all seemed rather vague and far away still, to me at least.

Some of the boys I knew were taking it seriously. Brian was one of them. He was nineteen, and he was giving up the course he had started, to join the army. We were having a Sunday picnic by the Yarra as a sort of farewell to him, because he was on final leave. There were about twelve of us. We had met at the beach and played tennis together since the previous summer. We often had casual parties on Saturday evenings, and danced to a record-player. Once somebody forgot to bring the records, so we danced all night to 'The Song of India'.

I liked Brian better than the other boys, but I tried not to show it. I thought he liked me too, because he danced with me most of the time.

141

It was a warm day at the end of spring when we were having this picnic. We had been riding on the somewhat ancient horses on the property, then some of the boys had swum in the river afterwards.

I had bought a film for my Kodak Brownie, and I wanted to put it in the camera and take photos of everyone sitting around waiting to have an early meal. There were chops cooking on a wire griller, and a billy perched on the fire on some forked sticks.

Brian said it was better to put in the film away from the sun. He held aside the long, screening fronds of a weeping willow, and we sat in the cool dimness while he wound the film onto the spool in the camera, turning it carefully until the warning black finger came up.

'There — "The moving finger writes; and having writ, moves on", ' he said, smiling.

'Omar Khayyam! I didn't know you liked poetry, Brian.' I was excited to have found out something that somehow altered my whole impression of him.

'Well, I do,' he admitted, 'and I even write it sometimes. But that's a secret. If I write any while I'm away, I'll send it to you, shall I?'

He leant towards me as he spoke, and I felt suddenly shy, because I knew from the look in his tawny-coloured eyes that he was going to kiss me. The merest brushing of mouth against mouth, but it made me feel breathless and different. Brian's eyes looked dark now, and serious, and the thick fronds of the willow were a curtain screening us.

But the others had started to call us. The sun would be going in behind a cloud soon, and I wouldn't be able to take any photos if we didn't hurry up.

We came out reluctantly, blinking in the bright blaze of the late afternoon sun. I felt embarrassed, as if they all knew what had happened, and I covered up by making a great fuss of taking their photos. Then Brian asked someone to take some of the two of us together.

142

'You'll send me those photos, won't you? Promise?' he asked later as we said goodnight.

I kept my promise, but they came back to me from the Middle East months later, those photos, in my envelope marked 'Return to Sender'. I had been expecting them, because I had started to read the Casualty Reports every day.

NEVER GO BACK

You should never go back, people say, to a place you have loved in your childhood. You will find it smaller and shabbier; you may even lose the magic with which you have invested it. Time, which has gilded your memories of the past, may have dealth harshly with the reality of them. Houses will have been altered, or no longer have their secret gardens and cubby houses. The whole centre of a city may have changed its character with so many people from foreign lands walking its streets, the exotic colours of their skins and the snatches of strange languages making it suddenly a city that could be anywhere in the world.

But this isn't so in Hobart — it is safe to go back. Each time I return there is so much that is left that I remember; there is still that leap of recognition in the blood.

True, there are new tall buildings springing up to compete with Mount Wellington against the skyline. There are one-way streets, and hotted-up cars that are raced down the steep hills to the waterfront late at night far too fast, their tyres squealing in protest as they skid around the corners. But there is still the charm of bright cottage gardens in front of small houses, spilling their flowers over the fences onto the pavements, blue lark-spurs, tumbling pink and mauve sweetpeas, and the golden cups of the Guinea flower. There are, too, many another species you cannot name; they are old-fashioned now, and you will not find them in a modern plant nursery. There is a great temptation to steal a few cuttings, or collect the seeds that are scattered on the wind.

The cottages themselves are preserved so carefully, with bright paint on the front doors and window frames, to contrast with the old stone or bricks. There are shining brass knockers, and freshly laundered lace curtains, and often the cosy comfort of a sleek cat sitting on the sun-warmed front step. Everything to show that the people who live there really care about this heritage from the past that they own.

When revisiting places I had loved and remembered, I approached cautiously. Some of them had been destroyed. Pulled down, crumbled away with the erosion of time, or even burnt.

'It looks a good day to drive up Mount Wellington,' I said to my husband on our last trip to Hobart. 'I wonder if you can still get lunch at The Springs? Do you remember that photo of me wearing my Molly-O hat for the last time, sitting on the front steps of The Springs guest house with the three old ladies?'

But when we asked the man at the garage he shook his head.

'Gone,' he said. 'Burnt down in the bad bushfire year, and never replaced. Some trouble with the permit. It's those Greenies, you know.'

I visited Lenna at Battery Point with great trepidation. I remembered beautiful old Lenna from the past, with its golden sandstone walls mellow in the afternoon sunlight, and its doric columns adding elegance to the upstairs and downstairs verandahs. I have happy memories of playing with the children at Lenna while my mother was there having a game of bridge or mahjong. Not all the memories are happy ones though. There was the awful day when I knelt beside the lily pond to touch a water lily. (Just touch, I don't *think* I was going to pick it. If I was, I deserved what happened.) I fell in.

The lily pond was terribly deep, I couldn't reach the bottom, and the lily stalks tangled with my legs. There was green slime, which got up my nose and in my mouth. I panicked completely, but I was dragged out, partly by the hair, by the resourceful young son of the house. He escorted me up the wide shallow steps of the verandah, and through the doors into the beautiful room where the grown-ups were playing cards. I stood there, dripping on the carpet. There was water weed in my hair, and water squelched out of my black patent shoes. I can still hear the cries of alarm and concern, and the quest to find Nanny.

Poor Nanny, who had left her two older charges for a minute to get a cup of tea. I was cold, and still recovering from my fright, but I was soon diverted from my misery by the novelty of having a bath in a strange bathroom. Nanny at Lenna was English, and had one of the most beautiful and soothing voices I have ever heard, and the most infectious laugh. It was a great joke to go home in a borrowed boy's jumper and a pair of boy's knickers.

You can stay at Lenna these days, but it is hard to get a booking there.

'There is a Japanese conference here at the moment,' they told me the first time I enquired. I tried to visualise Lenna invaded by dozens of sleek Japanese businessmen, but my imagination couldn't cope. It was difficult to make the decision whether to stay there or not, but when I finally did it was fine. Lenna is an elegant inn and still has a certain ambience to it.

It is true that part of the garden has disappeared these days to make way for the new wing, but the building itself is pleasant, in harmony with the original house. The tennis court has gone to make way for the parking area, but — 'But there's the lily pond!' I said to Peter.

A circular pond, with a small fountain in the middle, set between the old building and the new. I could see him looking at it doubtfully.

'Are you sure it's the same one?' he asked. 'It doesn't look very deep.'

And then I remembered. In the old days there was a second pond, down to the left of the tennis court. It was rectangular, with huge red and black fish moving slowly among the lily leaves.

'And *very, very* deep,' I said.

The little zoo is no longer there out on the Domain, but that is just as well. I might have been haunted there by the ghost of my shabby old Tasmanian Tiger, or still heard the roars of those other handsome tigers, so far from their native Bengal, and incarcerated behind the iron bars of their concrete prison.

There were places I visited that I remembered differently.

My memories of them were a bit skew-whiff, as my father was fond of saying. This was certainly so with the house in King Street when I stood and looked in the back gate, obligingly left open. Had someone taken a slice off the garden? When the hen house had existed, surely it hadn't been so close to the back door? There didn't seem enough space, either, for the garden to ever have contained that long white pergola, covered with wistaria, where my swing had hung from one of the beams.

On the other hand, looking at the back of the house, I could see why Mount Wellington had loomed over my childhood. I could remember that when the pebbled glass window of the upstairs bathroom was open, I could look out and imagine that if I stretched out I would be able to touch the mountain with my fingertips. And it doesn't seem impossible that I could do that even now, so closely does Mount Wellington brood over the top of King Street.

I don't believe you should never go back. You just have to be prepared, like Alice, for a looking-glass world, which looks very like the real world as far as you can see, 'only you know it may be quite different on beyond'.

THE JAGGED EDGE

I possess only one photograph of my maternal grandmother, and this photo has a jagged edge.

A sepia studio portrait, it shows her looking straight at the camera, unsmiling, enigmatic. Even though the picture has faded to a light brown, you can tell that my grandmother has very dark eyes and dark hair. She reminded me of someone when I came across her photograph recently, and then I realised who it was. She has a look of a painting I have seen of her great-great-grandmother, who was married to Richard Brinsley Sheridan.

It didn't occur to me that there was anything strange about my grandmother's photograph having a torn, jagged edge. I imagined that it had been damaged by being handled over the years, had cracked down the middle, and finally broken. It was kept in an old tin box of family photos, and I searched for the other piece of it, but it was missing.

Then, one day recently my sister was showing me her collection of old photographs, and she had a copy of that same photograph of our grandmother.

The same — right down to the jagged edge.

When I exclaimed over this, she said: 'Yes, didn't you realise mummy tore her father off the photograph?'

I should have known.

A studio portrait on stout cardboard is not easily damaged, or easily torn either, for that matter. What strong emotion of anger or resentment boiled up in my mother and caused her to mutilate that photograph, destroy that image of her father, leaving only the picture of her mother?

I wish I knew.

The old photograph which had always interested and intrigued me now assumed a new importance. I studied it, searching for some clue.

My grandmother is standing stiffly behind a carved chair, one hand resting on the back of it. She is wearing a dark jacket with puffed sleeves, and a trimming of jet beads. There is a small white frill at her neckline, and she wears a heavy cross on a chain around her neck.

Her husband is on her right, sitting on the edge of a table, gazing into the distance, turned slightly away from her. He holds an open book in one hand.

I know these things about him even though he isn't in my photograph, because my uncle in Canada sent me a photostat copy of that old portrait. Sent it little knowing what an item of interest it would be to me; how closely I would study it. He looks a handsome man with a pleasant expression. A likeable man. There are no clues here.

I take the few photographs that I have of my mother as a child, with her brothers and sister, and spread them on the table. There are no dates on them, or even names on the back, so I have to guess their ages. There is one of three of the five children. The eldest boy isn't in it, or the baby son. My mother looks about ten or eleven, she is still wearing socks. Her frock reaches to her knees, and her lace-edged pantaloons show beneath it. Although I think this is taken before her mother died, there is something in the way her eyes stare steadily at the camera, unsmiling, wise beyond their years, which shows me that she knows what lies ahead. Already she knows. She knows.

Nobody is nursing baby Kitty, who sits propped up in an armchair in the middle of the picture. Her hair is sparse, and stands up around her little pointed face in wispy curls. She is solemn, a little apprehensive. I remember that she is no longer the baby. There is another baby, Joe, the youngest, who must be very tiny at this stage.

The boy in the photograph must be Willy, about five, solemn and sweet in his sailor suit. Too solemn. But perhaps it is the photographer, huddled under a black cloth behind his camera, speaking to them in a muffled voice, who makes them look so apprehensive?

My mother was twelve when her mother died of tuberculosis as many another Sheridan had done. This may have been the cause of my mother's resentment towards her father. The family of five, a good Catholic family, must surely have helped to hasten the course of her mother's illness. The doomed woman may have resented her numerous pregnancies and the effort of coping with five children as she became progressively more unwell. My mother, by the age of twelve, may have sensed this. Perhaps it was discussed in her hearing, talked about among the servants. It might have been enough to turn an unhappy bewildered child against her father.

Then, when their mother finally died, the family was broken up. Another cause for sorrow and anger. The father, a bank manager, decided to keep the three boys with him to be looked after by a housekeeper and nurse, but the girls were sent away. My mother was lucky because she went to her mother's parents at Spencer Park. They loved her, and gave her a good education, but she missed the other children, especially little Kitty who went to be looked after by the Sisters at the Convent of Marie Réparatrice in Limerick, and eventually joined their Order.

I have only met one of my mother's family, my darling Uncle Willy in Canada. My husband and I flew there from New York for a weekend, and Uncle Willy and I talked non-stop about the past. We sat downstairs in the cabin of the yacht which was sailing down the Great Lakes. We had a cocktail shaker full of martinis, and I had a tape recorder turned on. We both cried, Uncle Willy and I, and it wasn't just the martinis. I wasn't used to them, and they were certainly strong, but I needed them that day to help break down the barriers when there were such sad and powerful things to discuss.

Uncle Willy told me how my mother came home occasionally for visits, and how he remembered her walking him to school, holding his hand and buying him a penny chocolate on the way. He made her walk right up to the school door with him, he was so proud of her.

'She had a fur coat y'know. Generally only actresses wore them in those days. She wanted to be an actress, a serious actress of course, it's in the blood, but the war came and stopped all that. She became a Queen Alexandra Nursing Sister and went to the Middle East where she met your father. Ah well...'

I must have drunk a couple of martinis before I was brave enough to ask Uncle Willy about the Sinn Fein.

That was probably the real cause of the rift between my mother and her father. He and the three boys joined the Sinn Fein in the days when it wasn't such an offence to do so, almost more of a sport, a protest about what the British were doing to their country, but not the terrible life and death struggle that it later became. Although there is one story my mother used to tell and Uncle Willy repeated about Uncle Joe swimming the River Liffey while being shot at by the Black and Tans.

'That was during The Troubles,' she said, and I noticed later that he used the same term, 'The Troubles'.

But my mother developed British loyalties, and must therefore have been emotionally torn to pieces.

It was when I mentioned the Sinn Fein that tears came into Uncle Willy's eyes. I cried too, and patted his hand as he told me he didn't approve of the things that were happening in Ireland these days, the innocent suffering with the guilty. He thought they had all gone mad, everything out of control. Across the sea in Canada, sailing down the Great Lakes, he shed tears for his native country and its war-torn people.

And that perhaps is the true cause of the jagged edge of my grandmother's portrait. Ireland. Ripped apart as ruthlessly as that photograph.

Whatever the cause, I am never going to learn the truth of it now. When I face up to things like this, I realise that although I always thought I was close to my mother, I really hardly knew her. She didn't like discussing her childhood, and as we had been brought up to have good manners we politely skirted around the subject, unless curiosity really got the better of us.

'Curiosity killed the cat,' we used to be told by various

maids who couldn't be bothered to answer when Bubba and I asked them questions. Perhaps as far as my mother's past was concerned it would have been better if we had kept nudging away at the barriers till we toppled them over. It would have been a relief to her, and far better for Bubba and me in later life when we tried to fill the gaps and found there was always something missing.

It is like one of those number puzzles you can buy that have an empty square.

Click, click, you think you have got it right, but there always seems to be a piece out of place. Click, click, there is always a piece missing.

May Flanagan, mother of Rita Giblin, Longford, Eire, 1891.

Bubba with a lion cub at Hobart Zoo, 1929.

IT GOES UP AND
THEN DOWN

'Perhaps you would like to read these childhood memories I have written down,' I said to Bubba the other day. 'After all, some of them are about you.' I was anxious to know what Bubba thought about the things I had written.

When she had finished reading them, Bubba seemed puzzled. 'How is it that I don't remember things happening the same way?' she said. 'I mean, some things I remember quite differently, and others I don't recall at all.'

I didn't know. Perhaps it was just because she was three years younger.

'Well, tell me some of the things *you* remember,' I said to her.

'The zoo. I remember the zoo differently. You seem to have been obsessed by the Tasmanian Tiger, but don't you remember the lion cub, Moi?'

She riffled through a box of old photographs until she found the one she wanted. Bubba, aged about four, sitting on a chair in a garden, with her legs tucked up under her. A half-grown lion cub is rubbing itself against the chair, its tail curling around the arm of the chair, looking for all the world like an outsize domestic cat. It has the triangular eyes and upward curving mouth which make lions appear to be such sweet-natured animals. Bubba has a rather set expression; she isn't nearly as relaxed as the lion cub. I remember this incident well now, although I had forgotten it. Perhaps I had been asked to be photographed with the young lion too, and hadn't been brave enough? It was clear to me early in life that Bubba was braver than I was, although she was three years younger. I was proud of her, but I was a bit jealous too.

The lion cub had been hand-reared by the Head Keeper when its mother had abandoned it. The keeper used to ask my father to have a cup of coffee when he saw us in the zoo on Sunday mornings, and the lion would be roaming loose in his garden. I was very frightened of it.

'Any chance of the Bengal tiger having cubs?' my father asked the Head Keeper one morning. My father just loved tigers.

'I don't think so. Tigers rarely breed in captivity,' he replied.

'A pity,' said my father.

I thought it was a very good thing. I could see what my father was up to. He was hoping there might be a spare tiger cub around some day, and wondering if there was any chance of getting his hands on it. He had visions of us hand-rearing it for a while on a bottle, and then returning it to the zoo before it got to the man-eating stage.

The more Bubba and I delved into the past, and sorted through faded photographs and old letters, the more differences we found in our memories of what had happened.

Bubba had forgotten about all the tall crimson poppies, splotched with blue, which we had found in the vegetable garden at Brighton. When we picked them a thick white milk oozed out of the stems.

'Hmm, *opium* poppies,' said my father when we ran inside with them. He showed them to my mother and said: 'What do you think of that, eh Rita?' He was very intrigued about Kelmer the Healer who had once lived in the house, and made his own remedies for his patients.

'Can't you remember dad hopefully sniffing the old blue and green bottles in the laundry to try to conjure up the ingredients in the Healer's potions?' I asked Bubba.

'What bottles?' she said.

But, on the other hand, I can't remember Bubba's birthday party when our father came into the room wearing an Egyptian tunic he had brought back from the Middle East. And he had on his head, she remembers, a cushion tied on with a cord. Her friends looked at him open-mouthed, and she felt embarrassed, but when he had sung a few songs and performed a couple of conjuring tricks, he had won them over. Although I can't remember that party, I can recall the conjuring tricks on other occasions. My father used to practise them so that he could divert small patients with them after they had received an injection. The penny that disappeared out of his hand, and reappeared when he rubbed his elbow, and the threepence that vanished from a matchbox. It was no ordinary matchbox; my father had bought it at a Magic Shop. They often went wrong, these tricks, but that was really better than when they were successful. We couldn't stop laughing, my father most of all.

'It's strange,' said Bubba, 'that I remember the past so differently to you. You'd think, wouldn't you, that if I were *there* when these things happened, my memories of them would be very close to yours?'

Perhaps, as I had already said to her, it was because she was three years younger than I was.

But I had the feeling too that although time tarnishes and fades things, time can also bathe the past in gold. From my golden childhood I can hear an echo of my father's words when he described the 'rassle-dassle' at the Exhibition of 1894, which could be a description of the whole of life:

'A thing like a roundabout only it goes round and as it goes round it goes up and then down and it keeps on like that...'